ROAD TO LOGISTICS

Shajith Naran

INDIA • SINGAPORE • MALAYSIA

ISBN 979-8-89233-340-5

Dedication

To my father, a beacon of strength and wisdom in my life. Your enduring love and unwavering guidance have been the true North Star of my journey. Just as a ship finds its way through treacherous waters by following the guiding light of the North Star, I have navigated the challenges of life with your lessons and values as my guiding light. Your sacrifices, your sacrifices, and your boundless love have been the compass that has directed my path. This book is a testament to the values you instilled in me and the lessons you've imparted along the way. It is a humble tribute to your enduring influence in my life.

To my Family, the cornerstone of my existence. Your support and understanding have been the sturdy foundation upon which I've built my dreams and aspirations. The love, encouragement, and warmth you've showered upon me have filled every page of my life's story with purpose and meaning. In every success I've achieved and every challenge I've overcome, your unwavering belief in me has been the driving force. This book is a celebration of the unity and strength of our family bond. It is a testament to the love that runs deep within our veins and the unbreakable ties that bind us together.

To my Mentors and Well-wishers, the guiding stars in my professional journey. Your wisdom, mentorship, and unshakable belief in my potential have not only illuminated my path but have also fuelled my aspirations. Your encouragement has propelled me to reach for the stars and to continually strive for excellence. This book stands as a tribute to your invaluable guidance and the profound impact you've had on my career. Your influence will forever echo in the choices I make and the success I achieve.

This book is dedicated to you, the beloved characters in the story of my life. Without your presence, your love, and your guidance, my journey would lack its heart and soul. It is my hope that the words within these pages convey the depth of my gratitude and the extent of my love for each one of you.

With boundless gratitude and love,

CONTENTS

Inclusion of Names 7

Preface 9

Gratitude 11

Book Recommendation 13

1. Birth of a Logistician 17
2. Career Lader 31
3. Became an Owner 45
4. Growth Addition 53
5. Breakup 60
6. Revenge 65
7. Accreditations 73
8. Dynamics 81
9. Back Home 90
10. Sabbatical 107

“YOU ARE NOT A
TRUE SUCCESS
UNLESS YOU’RE
HELPING OTHERS
BE SUCCESSFUL”

JON GORDON

INCLUSION OF NAMES

In the course of drafting my book, I initially secured explicit consent to feature the names of both the organizations I had the privilege to work with and the colleagues who contributed to my journey. However, as time has progressed, I've encountered a series of intricate legal considerations and evolving circumstances that have led me to reevaluate this initial approach.

Some names are actual as I obtained written consents to use their names in this book.

In contemplating the future publication of my book, I've felt compelled to make a significant alteration. Specifically, I have decided to obscure or anonymize the names of these organizations and colleagues throughout the narrative. This decision arises from a profound commitment to uphold strict legal compliance, an unwavering dedication to safeguarding the privacy and confidentiality of all individuals and entities involved, and a genuine desire to respect the boundaries set forth by consent agreements.

While this decision may necessitate adjustments to the overall presentation of my narrative, I firmly believe it is a critical step. It serves to ensure that the forthcoming publication adheres rigorously to the laws and regulations governing such matters, while also preserving the privacy and dignity of those who played a part in my journey.

PREFACE

The winding roads of the logistics industry have shaped my life and career over the past three decades. As I stand at the intersection of experience and expertise, I find myself compelled to share the incredible journey that logistics has taken me on. This book, " Road to Logistics," is the result of that inspiration.

The logistics isn't just a profession to me; it's a lifelong passion. From my earliest days as a sales executive to my current role as Chief Commercial Officer at family oriented Middle East logistics group, I've dedicated myself to understanding the intricate dance of supply chain, the art of problem-solving, and the constant evolution of this ever-important field.

Why write a book about Experience? The answer is simple: to share the wealth of knowledge I've gained, to offer a glimpse into the complex world of logistics, and to inspire those who are just beginning their journey in this industry. I believe that logistics is the beating heart of global commerce, and the lessons I've learned along the way are invaluable.

In the pages that follow, you'll find a mix of personal anecdotes, industry insights, and practical advice. Whether you're a seasoned logistics professional, an aspiring student, or simply someone intrigued by the intricate web that enables products to reach your doorstep, there's something here for you.

With each chapter, I hope to convey not only the technical aspects of logistics but also the excitement and passion that have fuelled my journey. This book is more than a collection of words; it's a testament to the belief that logistics, at its core, is about solving puzzles and connecting the world.

So, welcome to the "Road to Logistics." Buckle up, for we're about to embark on a journey through the twists and turns, the triumphs and tribulations, and the sheer beauty of logistics.

Let's begin.

GRATITUDE

I am filled with immense gratitude for the remarkable individuals who have been an integral part of my journey. Your unwavering support, guidance, and contributions have been instrumental in shaping the path that brought me to this moment.

To my colleagues in different organizations, you have been the driving force behind my professional growth. Each of you has brought your unique skills, perspectives, and enthusiasm to our shared endeavours. Your dedication and camaraderie have been a constant source of inspiration.

I must also extend my appreciation to those who posed challenges and negativity along the way. While these moments were not without their difficulties, they, too, have played a vital role in my personal and professional development. They have taught me resilience and the importance of embracing adversity as a catalyst for growth.

This book is a testament to the power of collaboration and the strength of the bonds we forge in our professional lives. Your presence in my journey has enriched my experiences, and I am deeply thankful for each one of you.

As I look ahead to future chapters, I do so with the knowledge that the connections and relationships formed in the past will continue to shape my path. To all my colleagues, mentors, collaborators, and even those who challenged me, thank you for being a part of my story.

BOOK RECOMMENDATION

I enthusiastically recommend "Road to Logistics: A True Experience" by Naran. This captivating book offers unique insights into the world of logistics, simplifying complex concepts for both industry professionals and newcomers. Naran's passion and dedication shine through, making it a must-read for those looking to deepen their understanding of logistics. Whether you're a seasoned professional or a curious newcomer, "Road to Logistics" is an invaluable resource that invites you into the industry. Kudos to Naran for his tremendous effort in sharing knowledge and enhancing our appreciation of this multifaceted field.

Having worked with Naran and being a part of this book, I can attest to his passion for the subject and dedication to excellence. His commitment to sharing knowledge and fostering a deeper understanding of logistics shines through in every chapter.

– Uwe

Ex colleague & Sr. Vice President

◆✱◆

"The Road to Logistics" is not just a book; it's a comprehensive experience that will undoubtedly serve as a reference guide for entrepreneurs and logistics professionals alike. Shajith has skilfully presented his memories in simple language, making the content easily understandable. This work is poised to become an invaluable resource, offering practical insights and a relatable narrative for those navigating the dynamic world of logistics.

– Nassar BP

President & CEO- Frontline Logistics Group.

◆✱◆

"Road to Logistics" by Shajith Naran is a book that breaks down complex logistics concepts into simple, relatable language. It's not your typical business guide; it offers a thrilling novel-like experience in the middle, complete with the satisfying taste of avenging injustice, just as any skilled sales expert would.

This book is a definite guide for new entrepreneurs who aspire to start a business in the GCC (Gulf Cooperation Council) region. It's not just informative; it's a captivating read that will keep you enthralled from start to finish. Shajith Naran has crafted a compelling narrative that combines the excitement of a thriller with valuable insights for budding entrepreneurs.

– Dr. Vivian Castellino

Chief Operating officer/Frontline Logistics

I am delighted to share my thoughts on "Road to Logistics," written by someone I had the privilege of working alongside in the early stages of his career. Having witnessed his growth.

The author's writing style is engaging and accessible, making even the most complex concepts understandable to readers from diverse backgrounds.

Having been a firsthand witness to the author's ups and downs, I can confirm that this book accurately reflects the challenges and successes that have shaped the industry. It serves as a valuable guide for those seeking to establish their presence in the field of logistics, offering profound insights and a well-defined roadmap to navigate the distinctive landscape of the sector in Middle east

– Santhosh. KV

Ex-Colleague

Reading "Road to Logistics" has brought me a great sense of happiness and pride. This book holds a special place in my heart because Shajith and I had multiple in-depth discussions during the final stage of this book,

The content of this book is not just another piece of literature; it's a valuable resource for those aspiring to make a mark in the logistics industry. It offers a comprehensive and insightful view of the field, addressing various aspects, challenges, and opportunities.

– Sunil Kumar

CHRO- Frontline logistics

◆✱◆

An exceptional book in taking your journey on the Road to Logistics, a must-read book for every person aspiring to be a logistician, I strongly recommend this book to every student of logistics as it provides a detailed narrative that bridges theory with the realities of life in the logistics industry.

This book 'The Road to Logistics' by Mr Shajith., serves as a mentor, guide and takes you on a journey through the intricacies of Supply chain and the freight Industry, this shall serve as companion that provides you with an enriching experience about the life and frail of a hardcore logistician.

Congratulate Shajith on this book, by getting into the detail by every minute, for the road to be taken. In Short: A must read book for every aspiring student of logistics.

– Mujeeb Rahman

Dean- Frontline Academy of logistics

◆✱◆

1

BIRTH OF A LOGISTICIAN

In 1993, life had begun to settle into a routine after I graduated. I had secured a job with a telecommunication company, and I was also juggling a computer course in the early hours of each day and an MBA correspondence program through Annamalai University's distant education program. The pursuit of education was never easy, especially during those times when getting admission into such courses was a significant challenge. However, my journey took an unexpected turn due to the influence of one of my father's close friends.

This friend, who held a special place in my father's life, played a pivotal role in helping me gain admission to the MBA program. Despite the daunting task of managing both my job at leading Mobile service provider in India and the demanding courses, I managed to pass with minimal marks, just enough to get by.

My career at this MSP was on an upward trajectory, and I had no intention of venturing abroad for work. It was during one of my routine marketing presentations for Mobile connection and equipment sales, aimed at securing a bulk booking from a travel company, that fate intervened. As I passionately pitched our services, I couldn't help but notice a tall, well-dressed gentleman observing me through the glass partition that separated the conference room from the MD's cabin.

This sharply dressed individual, clad in a white shirt, red tie, and a navy suit, exuded an air of sophistication. His impeccable choice of attire was complemented by tan shoes, a matching belt, and what appeared to be a valuable timepiece. Though I couldn't discern the brand or price of the watch, it left an impression.

To my surprise and slight embarrassment, this gentleman introduced himself as the Director of HR from a group of companies at Saudi Arabia. He explained that he had come to interview potential staff for one of their divisions engaged in the Cargo and Freight Forwarding industry. This was a world entirely foreign to me, and I had no inkling of what activities were involved in such an industry. Nevertheless, I nodded and tried to feign familiarity with the sector.

With a keen eye, he evaluated me silently, and I could sense my ego reaching its peak when he extended an unexpected job offer for a sales executive position. Despite my initial reluctance to work in the Middle East, I accepted his business card when he urged me to reconsider my decision. At that time, international calls were both challenging and expensive, so he suggested I send him a fax when I changed my mind.

Upon returning home, I shared the encounter with my family during dinner. My decision not to pursue this opportunity left my mother upset. She questioned why no one in her family had ever ventured to work in the Middle East and encouraged me to seize the chance. After a lengthy debate, my father too sided with my mother's viewpoint, and I reluctantly agreed to follow their wishes.

The next hurdle was creating a CV. In those days, computers and printers were rare, if not nonexistent, and I had to visit a typewriting center. Somehow, I managed to obtain a copy of my CV, but the real challenge was faxing it to Captain Jamal in the nearby city, which I accomplished after three days of anxiety and reluctance.

Much to my surprise, Captain Jamal received my fax and company where we had initially met. He also asked me to hand over my passport, which I dutifully did in the following month. Little did I know that this seemingly random encounter would mark the beginning of a life-altering journey, filled with unexpected opportunities and adventures beyond my wildest dreams.

This momentous decision marked a significant turning point in my life, propelling me into the world of logistics and freight forwarding. As I stepped into this new career path, I had no idea of the profound impact it would have on my personal and professional development.

On that fateful day in June 1994, as I stood at the threshold of my first-ever international journey, the mix of emotions swirling within me was palpable. I had dreamt of this day for so long, and now, finally, it had arrived. Saudi Arabia beckoned, a land of promise and opportunity, and I was determined to seize it.

The preparations had been meticulous. The travel company had assured me that my visa and ticket were ready for collection at their Mumbai office, which had only recently shed its colonial-era name of Bombay. To reach Mumbai, I embarked on an arduous journey by road, setting out on the evening of June 8th. Two days later, on June 10th, I found myself in the bustling heart of Mumbai, where I was warmly welcomed by relatives who graciously hosted me and my uncle who accompanied me.

The moment of reckoning, however, was at hand. I stepped into the travel agent's office with a heart full of hope and anticipation. But that hope quickly turned to disbelief as they presented me with a staggering bill - one lakh thirty thousand rupees - for the visa, stamping, and air ticket. My mind raced, struggling to reconcile this demand with Captain's reassuring words that this entire opportunity was to be provided free of charge. My uncle, who was a lawyer by himself, joined in my protestations, the two of us fervently quoting Captain's unequivocal assurances.

The atmosphere in the office grew tense as we debated the issue, with neither side willing to yield. Despite our passionate arguments, the travel company remained unyielding in their insistence on payment. Dejected and disheartened, we left the office, clutching the envelope of uncertainty that had just been thrust upon us.

Desperate for guidance and a solution, I turned to a relative who resided in Mumbai. Following his counsel, I hastily composed a fax to Captain Jamal, laying bare the entire ordeal and the unanticipated financial demand by the agent. With bated breath, I hit the send button and waited, my hopes hanging by a thread.

To my astonishment, the response came with astonishing speed. In a matter of just thirty minutes, Captain Jamal replied, his words etched with urgency, instructing me to remain where I was while he took action on my behalf. It was a glimmer of hope in a situation that had seemed hopeless just moments ago.

As I waited in the cramped telephone booth, the phone rang, sending a shiver down my spine. It was the travel company, their voices carrying a mix of sorrow and frustration. They lamented the complaint I had lodged against them and, in a surprising turn of events, offered to provide my passport and visa without any financial burden on my part. Their plea for me to return to their agency was earnest and heartfelt.

Although the circumstances were shrouded in mystery, I remained steadfast in my resolve to follow through with my planned journey. The date on which it had been scheduled, June 12th, loomed closer, and I was determined to step onto that plane and into the unknown.

Mixed emotions swirled within me as I contemplated the decisions that had led me to this point. Anticipation, excitement, and a profound sense of opportunity mingled with an unfamiliar fear that had crept into my consciousness. What awaited me in the Kingdom of Saudi Arabia, both in terms of personal growth and professional prospects, was a tantalizing question mark.

Finally, after a seemingly interminable 4.45-hour flight, the wheels of my plane touched down on the tarmac of this new land of hope and excitement. As I stepped off the plane at Dammam airport in the Kingdom of Saudi Arabia, my heart raced with a mix of anticipation and excitement. The unfamiliar surroundings, the buzz of the airport, and the realization that I was in a new and intriguing destination heightened my senses. It was a moment charged with the thrill of exploration, marking the beginning of a journey into the unknown and my passport clutched firmly in my hand. The journey had not been without its challenges, but I had overcome each one, one step at a time.

Navigating through immigration and customs became the next daunting task. The fear of making contact, the language barrier, and the uncertainty of how I would reach my final destination all weighed heavily on my mind. However, I found solace in the company of fellow travelers and the guidance of kind-hearted locals who, sensing my trepidation, extended a helping hand.

My first international travel experience had been nothing short of an emotional rollercoaster. From the initial thrill of anticipation to the shock of unexpected financial demands, from the resolve to stand by my decision to the uncertainty of what lay ahead – it had been a journey of self-discovery and resilience. Little did I know then that this voyage marked the beginning of a transformative chapter in my life, one that would shape my future in ways I could only begin to imagine.

Stepping into the receiving area at the airport, my heart raced with a combination of fear and excitement. The travel agent had assured me that someone would be waiting to pick me up, holding a placard with my name. As I scanned the crowd of people, including those dressed in traditional Arabic attire, all clutching name placards, I began my search.

To my surprise, I spotted not one but two placards bearing my name. The first board listed twelve names, including mine, while the second had only three names. Following my instincts, I hurried over to the second man with the smaller group. Just as I was about to join them, more passengers gathered around. The man, who appeared to be the organizer, issued instructions in Arabic, which I couldn't understand. However, I inferred his intentions from his gestures. Just as I was about to follow him, I noticed yet another placard, this one displaying only my name. Unfortunately, I wasn't allowed to approach him, leaving me stranded and unable to communicate.

Later, I learned that the man with many names had been sent by the Group Admin, the one with three names represented another department, and my own department had dispatched the man with my name alone.

As I followed the man from the Arab nation, we reached a Toyota vehicle with an extended cabin. He directed us to stow our luggage in the back and started driving. We traversed the desert for about 25 minutes and eventually arrived at a vast compound teeming with people from various countries. I realized that they hailed from multiple nations.

The driver handed us over to a Hindi-speaking supervisor who guided us to a large dining area. He instructed us to have our dinner, and once we finished, he led us to a room. To my shock, the room was shared by nine people, with three-tiered bunk beds and a decidedly unclean and unpleasant atmosphere. That night, I lay awake, cursing my luck and bemoaning the uncomfortable conditions.

The next morning, most of the people had left for work, leaving me with no instructions or information about my role or responsibilities. This continued for two days, leaving me feeling lost and isolated.

On the third day, I decided to approach the supervisor and seek answers. When I finally met him that evening, he appeared bewildered and asked why I was there, as I was not supposed to be in that camp; I was meant for the Cargo department. He quickly contacted the headquarters and administration, and within three hours, a car arrived to take me to HQ.

We arrived in front of an impressive seven-story building with the with huge hording of the company name emblazoned on it. It was a monumental structure unlike any I had ever entered before. There were two entrances, and I chose one and entered the reception area.

Inside, a spacious hall welcomed me, with a reception table where three black-clad Arab security personnel sat. The driver informed them about my arrival, and one of the security officers directed me to follow him. With my baggage in tow, I followed him, but midway, the main security office asked me to leave my luggage in a corner.

Continuing my journey, I reached the fifth floor, where I underwent the documentation process and surrendered my passport. Shortly after, a representative from the sixth floor arrived and guided me to the Cargo department. The entire sixth floor was dedicated to this department, bustling with around 150 or more people.

Without much delay, I was introduced to the Traffic Manager, Mr. Rouf, who had his hands in his pockets as he approached me. He introduced himself and Mr. Varghese, explaining that Varghese would be responsible for training me in sales. However, before diving into sales, I was to rotate through all the departmental functions, starting with scheduling, insurance, air freight, sea freight, and customs clearance more importantly in packing and moving department. After three months, I was slated to accompany Varghese for sales training.

As I stood there, bewildered by the complexities of the business and the whirlwind of new experiences, I couldn't help but wonder what lay ahead in this daunting journey in the world of international cargo and logistics.

The first day on the sixth floor of the massive building went surprisingly smoothly. I was introduced to a multitude of staff members, and they extended their support and camaraderie to me, recognizing that I was new not only to the industry but also to their country. It was a comforting feeling, knowing that I had allies in this foreign land.

Before leaving the office that day, I received a call from HR, instructing me to meet with Mr. Ebrahim, a kind-hearted gentleman from Egypt. He handed me 20 Saudi riyals and a sizable carton filled with essential items: two glass plates, two mugs, a tea pot, one pillow, two bed sheets, and a large blanket. Mr. Ebrahim also assigned one of his subordinates to assist me in transporting all these items to my living quarters.

I arrived at my new residence, a neatly arranged flat with three spacious rooms and a comfortable living area. As I entered one of the rooms, I found two beds neatly made up. It was in this room that I first met my roommate, Mr. Arshad, who hailed from Bihar and worked as a sales executive.

In just a few short hours, Arshad and I formed a close bond. We delved into discussions about our respective roles, the intricacies of the business, and our experiences thus far. Arshad was quick to offer his assistance and promised to guide me in acquiring a deeper understanding of the relocation business. His warmth and willingness to help eased any lingering anxieties about my new surroundings, and I felt grateful for the friendship that was already blossoming in this foreign land.

My office hours followed a unique schedule. We worked from 7:30 in the morning until 12 noon, and then resumed work from 3:30 in the afternoon until 6:00 in the evening. On the second day of my employment, I made sure to arrive promptly at 7:00 am, ready to tackle the challenges of the day. I settled into a couch, awaiting further instructions.

Mr. Rouf, my traffic manager, arrived shortly after and guided me to meet Mr. Kasar, who was responsible for managing all scheduling related to relocation, packing, and moving. I took my seat in front of him, but he seemed engrossed in his morning tasks, fielding numerous phone calls. After about 20 minutes, he handed me a stack of documents and instructed me to make photocopies, asked me neatly stapling them together in sets and return.

Although I didn't voice my frustration, I couldn't help but wonder if this was the kind of work I had signed up for after completing my MBA. This routine persisted throughout the week, with Mr. Kasar never making an effort to provide guidance or instruction. Instead, I was left to decipher the information from the documents on my own. Fortunately, I had a newfound friend in Mr. Santhosh, who handled all matters related to insurance coordination. In our native language, he took it upon himself to explain the intricacies of the job to me. Our bond grew strong during this time, and to this day, we maintain a close friendship, meeting regularly and sharing memorable moments at parties.

My next assignment was in the Air Export department, a role that proved to be quite challenging. I had to learn the codes of various airlines, airport codes, and understand the different procedures associated with each airline. Additionally, I had the responsibility of generating live Airway

Bills (AWB), which was a demanding task for a novice like me. However, I had a reliable guide in Mr. Antony Gavino, a short, friendly Filipino national who supported me wholeheartedly and generously shared his knowledge.

Following my stint in the Air Export department, I transitioned to the Sea Export department, where I encountered another Filipino colleague. While he wasn't as forthcoming as others, he stressed the importance of understanding the nuances of this area for a Salesperson like me.

One morning, in the midst of my rotations, Mr. Rouf called me and inquired if I was ready to handle the Airfreight desk. I affirmed my readiness, and he entrusted me with the responsibility as Mr. Antony had to take emergency leave due to his father's passing. This marked a significant step in my journey, as it was an opportunity to prove my capabilities in a role of greater responsibility within the company.

As I faced the daunting responsibility of managing the Air Export department during Mr. Antony's two-month emergency leave, a whirlwind of emotions churned within me. Fear, anxiety, and confusion gripped me, but deep down, I possessed an unyielding instinct to rise to the occasion. With little more than a week's worth of experience in the department, I knew it was a colossal task ahead of me.

Mr. Antony, recognizing my determination, took it upon himself to provide me with as much information and shortcuts as possible to help me navigate this unfamiliar terrain. Little did I know that this well-intentioned guidance would eventually lead me to make one of the gravest mistakes in my career as a logistician.

The days were a blur of constant activity. Managing 30-40 Airway Bills (AWBs) at a day, ensuring all the necessary documents were in order, liaising with the scheduling department, booking with airlines, sending pre-alerts, closing files, and forwarding them to the accounts department – the workload was overwhelming. I relied heavily on the support and guidance of my colleagues to get through each day.

Amidst this chaotic period, I found myself tasked with handling the remains of a Nepali citizen late one evening. I hadn't received any prior training for such an event, but remembered Antony's words and shortcuts. Unfortunately, this time, my overconfidence led to a catastrophic error. In the cargo description column of the Master Airway Bill (MAWB) for the dead body, I mindlessly copied the description from a previous AWB, which had been prepared for spare parts being sent to Bentley Navada, Canada. In that column, I typed "Repair and return" without fully comprehending the gravity of my mistake. I proceeded to prepare the supporting documents, staple the AWB pouch, and sent the entire package to the Scheduling department. The body was to be transported to the airport from the hospital, accompanied by the AWB and pouch.

The following morning, as I arrived at the office around 7:15 am, I was met with a gathering of managers, including GM, Mr. Kamal and Rouf. My immediate manager's face was flushed with anger, and GM Siddawi regarded me with a perplexed expression. Raouf demanded to know where I intended to send a deceased body for repair. It was at that moment that a jolt of realization hit me like lightning, and my vision darkened. When I regained my composure, the enormity of my error became painfully clear – I had unwittingly disrespected a departed soul. I braced myself for the consequences, expecting my journey to end abruptly, either through termination or a one-way ticket home.

Santhosh, my trusted friend and colleague, later informed me that customs clearance department had spotted the mistake early that morning before dispatching the body to the airport. Raouf had promptly made the necessary corrections. While I escaped termination, I received my first warning letter within a month's my joining. This incident, while humiliating, also served as a powerful lesson, strengthening my resolve to learn and grow.

I began dedicating more time to preparing AWBs and documents. I delved into older files, taking meticulous notes and learning from each experience. When faced with a new type of export, I reached out to the accounts department to acquire a similar job file for reference, ensuring a more careful approach. Despite my meticulous efforts, I would go on to make further mistakes, including sending diplomatic cargo to Minneapolis instead of Miami, which had a significant impact on my career.

However, during this tumultuous period, I forged strong relationships with GM Kamal and Raouf by teaching them computer operations and assisting with proposals and database management. Despite the setbacks, these experiences shaped me into a more resilient and knowledgeable logistics professional. I now share these stories with the new generation of logistics professionals as valuable case studies, emphasizing the importance of diligence and attention to detail in our field.

During my two months at that company, two significant events occurred that left a lasting impact on my experience there. The first was the encounter with Captain Jamal, and the second was the joint venture agreement signed between our company and a prominent American player in the freight forwarding industry at that time.

One memorable afternoon, as I was making my way up to the 6th floor, the elevator doors opened on the 2nd floor, and to my surprise, Captain Jamal stepped inside. We struck up a conversation, and I couldn't resist sharing with him my observation about the exorbitant fees charged by a particular travel company to candidates seeking employment. These charges included visa fees and ticket expenses, which seemed unjust.

That very afternoon, a memo from the Human Resources department made an announcement that all individuals who had arrived in the company through this specific travel agency should convene on the 5th floor. During the meeting, Captain Jamal delved into the matter, carefully questioning each attendee and confirming the amount of money that had been collected from them by the travel agency.

In an act of solidarity and transparency, approximately 34 individuals, as per my recollection, provided details on a common sheet of paper. Later, I learned that thanks to Captain Jamal's intervention, these employees were able to recover the money they had paid to the agent. However, the travel agency faced severe consequences, as its actions led to the suspension of their partnership with our organization, thereby landing them on the company's blacklist.

This incident showcased the company's commitment to its employees' welfare and highlighted the influential role Captain Jamal played in ensuring justice prevailed. It was a testament to the values and principles upheld by the company and its leadership, leaving a profound impression on my experience during my tenure with the company.

The expansion of new joint venture into Saudi Arabia marked a significant development during my time at here. They established their office on the 6th floor of the same building, initially with just one employee transferred from their Dubai office. However, they were in need of additional manpower in Saudi Arabia to support their growing operations.

Around one month after the inauguration the corporation in Saudi Arabia, Mr. Siddawi summoned me to his office on the 7th floor. As I promptly arrived and entered his office, he informed me of a pivotal change in my role. Instead of continuing in my position as a Sales Executive in Relocation Sales, I was to transition to a new role under the joint venture's payroll. This new role focused on freight forwarding, which involved a different set of responsibilities compared to the activities typically associated with a packing and moving company.

I embraced this opportunity and began a deep dive into learning the intricacies of the freight industry. Over time, Mr. Raouf shared with me the company's plans to send me to the new branch in Riyadh.

After two months of preparation, the day arrived when it was officially announced that I would be transferred to the Riyadh office. This move came with a slight hike in my current hierarchy, effectively marking my first promotion and salary structure. I felt a surge of excitement and anticipation as I embarked on this new chapter in my career.

Upon my arrival in Riyadh, I was introduced to Mr. Jean, a figure known as terminator for his strict and demanding demeanor. Santhosh had warned me before leaving Dammam that surviving under Mr. Jean would be a significant challenge, as very few employees managed to stay with him for more than two years.

During the subsequent five years, I was resolute in my determination to prove myself and leave a lasting impression in Riyadh. This period was marked by a rollercoaster of experiences, with both highs and lows that tested my resilience and adaptability.

Under Mr. Jean leadership, I faced various challenges and opportunities. Despite the initial difficulties, I managed not only to survive but also to thrive in this dynamic environment. One of the most significant achievements during this time was the development of a strong rapport with Mr. Bustani himself. Our professional relationship grew stronger as we worked together, and I learned valuable lessons from his leadership style and expertise.

Moreover, I achieved several remarkable milestones and accomplishments during these five years. These successes were the result of hard work, dedication, and the valuable experiences I gained along the way. They were a testament to my ability to navigate the complexities of the professional world in Riyadh and make a meaningful impact.

This period of my career was characterized by growth, both personally and professionally. It reinforced my determination and resilience, helping me build a strong foundation for my future endeavours in Riyadh and beyond

My time in Riyadh proved to be a significant milestone, laying a solid foundation and equipping me with a wealth of knowledge and experiences in the freight forwarding industry. I look forward to sharing these experiences with newcomers, as I believe they can provide valuable insights and guidance to those embarking on their own careers in this dynamic field.

In 1998, while employed in in Riyadh, I encountered a truly harrowing experience that unfolded unexpectedly. As our routine operations involved the successful transportation of a shipment moved from Colombo to Riyadh through the Dammam Sea port. The process included forwarding from Colombo to Riyadh on FOB basis, clearing the customs, delivering the goods to the consignee warehouse, and returning the emptied container to the shipping line, all in accordance with our standard responsibilities. The shipment, containing wooden doors, seemed like just another ordinary task. However, what followed was far from routine. As events unfolded, it became clear that this seemingly mundane process was about to take a terrifying turn, plunging me into a situation I had not anticipated during my time in the freight forwarding industry.

Two weeks later, as I entered the office one morning, I was met with a scene of heightened tension - police vehicles surrounded the premises, and officers were scattered around. The gravity of the situation became apparent as an unsettling atmosphere loomed. Despite the ominous signs, I made my way to my desk, only to be swiftly summoned by the Admin Manager. Upon entering his cabin, I found a group of high-ranking officers engaged in intense discussions in Arabic. The seriousness of the situation deepened as it became evident that the focus was on the shipment we had facilitated. My regional manager, Mr. Jean, was also present, and the interrogation in Arabic left me bewildered, struggling to comprehend the unfolding events. The air of uncertainty and the language barrier heightened the intensity of the situation, leaving me in a state of anxious perplexity.

Around 9 o'clock in the morning, we were taken to the Riyadh Police headquarters, an imposing and intimidating place that struck fear into my core. The uncertainty of the situation compounded my anxiety as I contemplated the potential consequences. The interrogation was rigorous, conducted in Arabic, leaving me in a state of heightened apprehension. Thankfully, a translator was provided to convert the inquiries into Hindi, easing the communication barrier. The experience was truly harrowing, the memory of it still evoking a visceral reaction. Fortunately, through the grace of God, my responses aligned with Mr. Jean's statements, and the personnel from the shipping line corroborated our accounts. After an intense and nerve-wracking ordeal that stretched until 11 o'clock that night, we were eventually granted permission to leave, bringing a profound sense of relief and gratitude for the alignment of our testimonies.

The day following our unsettling evets with the Saudi police, the reason for our ordeal began to unravel. It was revealed that the container we had diligently handled and transported from Colombo to Riyadh had been implicated in drug smuggling. The shocking revelation sent shivers down my spine. The ingenious method employed by the smugglers involved concealing drugs within the perforated hollow inner wall of the container, expertly welded to evade detection. This clandestine technique allowed the illegal cargo to pass through multiple customs inspections thru many countries unnoticed, adding a layer of sophistication to the illicit operation. The gravity of the situation dawned on us as we realized our unwitting involvement in a highly organized and covert criminal activity. The incident served as a stark reminder of the intricate challenges faced in the freight forwarding industry and the potential for unforeseen and perilous complications.

The unravelling of the drug smuggling operation occurred during the offloading process at Dammam port, a critical juncture in the journey of the container from Riyadh dry-port to its final destination. The ground support team, responsible for overseeing the meticulous logistics, astutely observed an irregularity in the weight distribution of the container. The realization that one side of the container bore an additional and unexpected load raised red flags, although such subtle nuances were typically overlooked in routine operations. Recognizing the potential gravity of the situation, the ground support team promptly notified the port authorities, and the customs officials were immediately alerted. It was a surreal and troubling experience, a situation we had no control over despite our best efforts.

The incident served as a poignant reminder of the inherent risks embedded in the freight forwarding industry and underscored the imperative for heightened security measures. The stressful and fearful experience prompted a revaluation of our protocols and a recognition of the ever-present threat of criminal activities infiltrating even the most diligent processes.

Amidst the turmoil, there was a silver lining in the form of cooperative efforts with the authorities. Gratitude emerged for the collaboration that unfolded during the investigation, where truth ultimately prevailed. The incident highlighted the critical importance of transparency and cooperation between industry stakeholders and law enforcement to safeguard against unforeseen criminal activities.

This unsettling event left an indelible mark, fostering a deeper understanding of the challenges faced by those in the freight forwarding sector. It reinforced the need for continuous vigilance, adaptation to evolving tactics employed by criminals, and a commitment to implementing robust security measures. In the face of adversity, the experience served as a catalyst for a renewed dedication to ensuring the integrity and security of the freight forwarding processes to prevent such incidents from recurring in the future.

2

CAREER LADER

My journey in the corporate world has been marked by a burning desire for personal and professional growth, reminiscent of the swift and sometimes daring decision-making style of Jean. Like many others in the corporate realm, I longed to break free from constraints and ascend to new heights.

During my seven-year tenure at Bax Global, I had the privilege of representing the company at four international conferences. These experiences were pivotal in my career and personal development, providing me with a wealth of knowledge and insights that enriched both aspects of my life.

Among the many memorable moments from those conferences, there is one amusing incident that stands out, and I'm eager to share it.

At one of these conferences, the setting was a grand and prestigious venue. People from various corners of the globe had gathered to discuss industry trends and exchange ideas. During one of the formal dinners, I found myself seated next to a distinguished delegate from a country known for its elaborate and formal dining etiquette.

As the meal progressed, I realized that I was struggling to navigate the complex array of cutlery and glasses arranged before me. It seemed like there were more utensils than I had ever seen at a dining table. With each course, my anxiety grew, and I discreetly observed those around me, trying to mimic their movements.

In a humorous turn of events, I inadvertently knocked over a wine glass with my elbow while attempting to gracefully partake in a toast. The entire table fell silent for a moment, and I could feel my face flush with embarrassment. However, my neighbour from the etiquette-focused country, rather than displaying irritation, burst into laughter. This unexpected reaction broke the tension, and soon, the entire table was chuckling along with us.

This incident taught me that even in formal and unfamiliar situations, a good sense of humour and a willingness to laugh at oneself can bridge cultural differences and create bonds. It became a memorable icebreaker, and throughout the conference, we shared many more laughs and stories, fostering a genuine connection with my fellow delegate.

In retrospect, this amusing mishap not only lightened the atmosphere but also highlighted the importance of humility and the ability to find common ground, even in the most unexpected situations. It was a valuable lesson in both cultural awareness and the power of laughter to forge connections in the professional world.

I remember another humorous incident In November 1996, I embarked on my maiden official trip to Hong Kong, where I was scheduled to attend the Bax Asia conference. It was my very first conference experience, and I was filled with excitement. I checked into a luxurious five-star hotel located in the scenic Colone area, near the sparkling waters of Hong Kong—a city renowned for its iconic bridges.

Exhausted from my journey, I arrived at the hotel around 6:30 in the evening and promptly fell into a deep slumber. When morning came, I awoke with a ravenous appetite, craving a substantial breakfast to kickstart my day. Without realizing it, I placed an order for breakfast from room service, unaware that my hotel booking included complimentary breakfast at the hotel's restaurant. I perused the menu and, spotting "American Breakfast," placed my order. To my surprise, the person on the other end of the line inquired, "How would you like your steeks, just done, half or full done?"

Now, bear in mind that this was my very first experience ordering breakfast at a five-star hotel, and I was overcome with a mix of curiosity and a touch of ego. Not fully comprehending the question, I confidently responded, "Just done." After a thirty-minute wait, breakfast arrived at my doorstep. To my dismay, the plate was adorned with what seemed like raw beef steaks, oozing with blood. It was quite the sight, and I hesitated to dig in.

I immediately called room service to express my concerns, and the person on the other end calmly explained, "You ordered it 'just done,' sir." Not wanting to make a fuss, I decided to skip the questionable beef steaks and enjoyed the other items on my plate. It was a culinary adventure I hadn't quite anticipated.

Later, during the conference, I shared this comical mishap with a colleague from Dubai, originally hailing from Kerala. He couldn't contain his laughter and kindly enlightened me about my breakfast blunder. It was then that I realized my own ignorance in the world of gourmet dining. This incident, rather unexpectedly, turned me into a keen observer of food, leading me to develop a deep passion for cooking and a voracious appetite for learning about cuisines from around the globe.

During my time with Bax, the first four years were incredibly frustrating when it came to staying in touch with my home country, especially between 1994 and 1996. Back then, making international calls was a real ordeal. We had to arrange for coins, known as halala, and then wait in line outside the coin booth to use the phone. It was quite a hassle. Thankfully, things improved when they replaced the coin system with cards. Just imagine how lucky the new generation is!

Technology has come a long way since then. Nowadays, with smartphones and the internet, staying connected internationally is so much easier. We can instantly message, make video calls, and use various digital communication tools that are far more convenient and cost-effective than those old phone booths.

It's really amazing how much things have changed, and I can't help but think that the younger generation today is incredibly fortunate to have these modern communication options. The world has become much smaller and more interconnected thanks to these rapid technological advancements.

During that period, there was a moment when I communicated with my father, and during our conversation, he shared the news of my success in an examination I had taken for the position of a veterinary assistant with the Public Service Commission (PSC), a state government body. To my surprise, his advice was for me to return and join government service, specifically in the role of a veterinary assistant, for which I had been selected by the PSC.

The decision to participate in the examination had not been my choice; I had done it under heavy pressure from my family. In all honesty, it wasn't a career I had initially set my heart on. My mind set was never go with a profession like that, even though every profession has its own dignity and respect.

However, as time passed and I immersed myself in this new profession as a logistician, something began to change within me. I found myself gradually enjoying the work and discovering a certain charm within it. It was as if I was starting to forge a genuine connection with the role, despite my initial reservations.

This experience led me to contemplate whether destiny might have played a part in this journey. Perhaps, against my initial wishes, this career was meant for me. It served as a valuable lesson that life can sometimes take us down unexpected paths, and we may discover our true calling in the most unlikely of places.

Ultimately, I came to realize the importance of listening to my own heart and instincts. Pursuing a career that resonates with me, even if it hadn't been my first choice, brought about a deeper sense of fulfilment and satisfaction.

As I continue to navigate the corporate landscape, my desire for growth burns brighter than ever. Each experience, whether humorous or challenging, contributes to my journey of self-improvement and helps me become a more well-rounded and culturally aware individual. And who knows, perhaps one day, I'll look back on these moments with the same wisdom and fondness that Jean's bold decisions have left in his wake, as I too strive to leave my mark on the world.

Amidst the ups and downs of my journey, a significant and wonderful chapter unfolded when I got married. My life took a meaningful turn as a remarkable partner entered it. Up until that point, most of my personal decisions had been made independently. However, now, there was someone by my side who became an integral part of my growth and decision-making process.

Many critical decisions were made with her unwavering support and wise counsel. I can confidently say that having a supportive and understanding wife is a true blessing. It's a partnership that extends beyond just sharing the good times; it's about having someone who stands with you, unwaveringly, even in the most challenging of situations.

Through the highs and lows of life, having a life partner who offers unwavering support and understanding is a source of immense strength and comfort. It's a reminder that in our journey, the presence of a loving and supportive companion can make all the difference.

My journey took an unexpected turn when I received valuable information from Santhosh about a German Logistics company, a subsidiary of German govt organization, planning to establish a branch in Dammam. They were in search of a strong candidate to fill the role of Operations Manager, requiring 5-10 years of experience. Without hesitation, I promptly sent in my application along with my CV. To my surprise, just four days later, I received a call from them inviting me for an interview with Mr. Uwe, the Managing Director of Saudi Arabia.

Reached at the appointed place on time and met Mr. Uwe, an imposing figure with magnetic eyes and a warm smile. Our conversation spanned various topics, ranging from industry-related matters to personal experiences. However, the real challenge lay ahead when he handed me a four-page questionnaire filled with technical questions. These questions covered a wide range of topics, from geology and container dimensions to loading diagrams, loading volume, types of airlines, incoterms, and pricing calculations for air and sea freight. It was no walk in the park, and did my best to provide answers. However, the bar was set high, requiring a score of 70% to secure the position, and managed to score only 60%. I left their office feeling disheartened, thinking that my opportunity had slipped away.

To my relief, a few days later, received a call from their HR department, informing me that the initially selected candidate had fallen through, and the next chance was being extended to me. This was a lifeline which desperately needed for my career growth. Without hesitation, I submitted my resignation to Bax, my current employer. I was fortunate to have a good relationship with Jean, who chose to terminate my employment instead of accepting the resignation. This strategic move allowed me to join the German company without any industry-related restrictions.

Informed to the new company about my situation, and they agreed to delay my start date by two months, during which I returned to my home country. After the stipulated period, made my way back to Dammam and officially assumed the role of Operations Manager. It was a significant step forward in my career, and was grateful for the turn of events that had brought me to this point.

I've learned a valuable lesson from this experience that I want to pass on to the new generation of logisticians and job seekers. When appearing for an interview with a corporate organization, it's essential to be well-prepared with product knowledge and the ability to convey that knowledge effectively to the interviewer. Many candidates may possess excellent knowledge but fail to articulate it during the interview. Remember, when you step into that interview room, one of two outcomes will occur: you will either gain the opportunity you seek or not. So, be bold, confident, and well-prepared when facing such circumstances, as you never know where a single interview might lead you on your journey of professional growth and success.

Impressing the person sitting in front of you during an interview is crucial, especially when you have limited knowledge in a particular area. It's not just about what you know; it's about how you present yourself. Transforming the interview into an interactive discussion is a significant part of succeeding in the process.

Most interviews tend to be one-way, with the interviewer asking questions and the candidate responding. However, when you turn it into an interaction, it opens up a broader space for meaningful discussion. This shift allows both parties to exchange valuable information and ideas. This not only helps you stand out but also creates a personal connection with the interviewer, increasing your chances of winning the interview.

Throughout my life, I've had numerous opportunities to create such situations as a candidate. Many times, I've approached interviews with the intention of fostering interaction rather than simply answering questions. Interestingly, I've also been on the other side, as a hiring manager, where candidates with this interactive approach have left a lasting impression. It's a strategy that can significantly enhance your chances of success in the interview process.

Indeed, in the logistics industry, rapid and genuine career growth often relies heavily on individual performance, smart work, and decision-making capacity. While personal relationships and recommendations can be helpful in various fields, logistics demands a unique set of skills and abilities.

Time management stands out as a critical benchmark for a successful logistician. Everyone has the same 24 hours in a day, but the true art lies in how effectively you manage those hours to maximize productivity and impact both customers and management positively. Success in this regard becomes the fuel that propels your career ladder closer to the top of the hierarchy.

In the logistics world, where precision and efficiency are paramount, mastering time management is not just a skill but a fundamental necessity.

It's the key to meeting deadlines, optimizing processes, and ultimately achieving remarkable career growth. While relationships can open doors, it's one's ability to consistently deliver results that truly distinguishes a logistics professional.

My tenure of 2 years as an Operations Manager, overseeing a team of around 10 individuals, was an enriching experience that I deeply valued. The success of my team was interwoven with my own accomplishments, and I made sure to maintain a positive and cooperative relationship with Uwe. Uwe's impressive sales strategies kindled my interest in the sales field, and my ambition knew no bounds. I aspired for continuous growth, mirroring my role model, Jean.

Recognizing that my growth potential in operations was limited, likely reaching a ceiling at the Operations Manager level, I yearned for more. I shared my desire to venture into sales with Uwe, who graciously allowed me to explore this avenue. Over the course of a year, I successfully acquired numerous customers, broadening our client base.

During this period, this German giant secured a pivotal project for a Saudi oil and gas organization. This project was of monumental importance to them and necessitated my involvement as the primary point of contact. I found myself making multiple trips to Germany to engage in discussions and finalize the intricate logistics involved in the massive and high-stakes lift movements, as well as the associated paperwork.

This experience added another feather to my cap, and I embraced the challenge with enthusiasm and dedication, fully aware of the significance of this project to both our company and our valued client.

In the realm of project forwarding, my earlier emphasis on time management should be revised. In this field, the dedication of 24 hours a day to work is often a necessity. Even the smallest oversight can result in millions of dollars in losses and significant damage. Precise timing and the on-time placement of heavy-lift cargo are paramount. Whether it's the delivery of a relatively small shipment or a massive project, timeliness is non-negotiable.

In this challenging environment, we cannot predict the exact arrival of vessels or flights, but we must be prepared to make the necessary arrangements to clear goods promptly. This involves obtaining approvals for clearance and road movement, securing escorts and road permits, and sometimes even dealing with road closures that last for hours. In extreme cases, it might be necessary to demolish and rebuild gates and may build new roads to accommodate oversized cargo and its smooth movement.

Additionally, conducting thorough pre-route surveys is a critical component when determining pricing. Without this essential step, the potential for significant losses increases substantially. Many days may require sacrificing sleep, and at times, one may find themselves sleeping in a truck or car to ensure that tasks are completed. In essence, succeeding in the field of project forwarding is far from easy; it demands unwavering dedication, meticulous planning, and the ability to adapt to unpredictable challenges.

It's not uncommon to hear that those who manage projects have the potential to generate additional income, whether through legitimate means or otherwise. In my own experience, I found this to be true. I was able to earn a significant amount of extra income through my involvement in this particular project, which surpassed what I had earned through years of dedicated effort in other roles.

I firmly believe in transparency and honesty, and I have no reservations about sharing this insight with my successors or colleagues. It's essential to acknowledge that certain projects or positions may present unique opportunities for financial gain, and it's important to navigate such situations ethically and within the boundaries of legal and professional standards. Successors can benefit from understanding the dynamics of the industry and the potential for additional income while ensuring that they maintain the highest standards of integrity and compliance in their endeavors.

During one of our project discussions, my German colleague and Project Director, Mr. Forintos, brought up an interesting challenge. We were dealing with smaller cargos that were intended to be shipped in shippers' own containers to reduce warehouse charges. The final destination in Saudi Arabia was a vast, open desert where, storing cargo was neither feasible nor secure. Therefore, we needed warehouse facilities, which incurred significant costs, especially over an extended period.

To address this issue, we decided to explore the possibility of containerizing the smaller-sized cargo. However, this introduced a new set of challenges, particularly concerning re positioning the containers once they were emptied. The containers themselves were worth approximately \$1000 in Germany, and if we were to send them back from KSA, it would incur substantial additional costs. This predicament led us to brainstorm various solutions.

In the midst of these discussions, one of my transport contacts mentioned that he knew someone who specialized in buying and selling shipping containers. Interestingly, this individual had been involved in supplying containers to the UN military in Iraq, where they were used to fortify compound walls by filling them with sand, providing a measure of protection against bomb explosions.

This revelation sparked new possibilities for us to address the container-related challenges we were facing in our project. It highlighted the importance of resourcefulness and thinking outside the box when encountering complex logistical issues. Finally I was authorized to deal with that and sell out the container with $ 1000 per container regardless of 20feet or 40feet, but of them were 40ft.

In my pursuit to address the container-related challenges we were facing in our project, I reached out to Mr. Hashim Ansari, a Pakistani national who had expertise in buying and selling shipping containers. As a negotiator and a businessman, I was armed with information from the shipping line regarding container prices in Iraq. Starting the negotiation at $4,000, we engaged in a series of discussions and bargaining sessions.

Ultimately, Mr. Ansari agreed to purchase the containers at a price of $3,000 per container. Instead of immediately informing Michel, I decided to report this development to Uwe, seeking his guidance. his response was intriguing. He mentioned that we were making substantial profits from this project and suggested a specific formula that can be benefitted for the team members on hierarchical basis and the company.

However, it's worth noting that he declined to take any portion of the contribution himself, citing personal ethics as his reason. The financial aspect of this trade was conducted entirely in cash, with no formal record-keeping required. It's important to clarify that this arrangement was made with what can be seen as the tacit approval of my boss, and I want to emphasize the significance of ethics when dealing with such situations. And this type of extra efforts was legalized by authority.

This story underscores the importance of maintaining ethical standards, even in challenging business scenarios. While the situation may have had its complexities, adhering to ethical principles is paramount, especially in the business world where trust and integrity play significant roles in building long-lasting relationships and a solid reputation.

Over the course of two years, as the project neared completion, my work schedule began to ease, and my aspirations for professional growth became more prominent. I had my sights set on the position of Branch Manager in Dammam, and eagerly awaited the opportunity for this designation. Despite shouldering the responsibilities associated with the role, the official title continued to elude me.

My next career goal was firmly fixed on that position. During this time, Uwe, who had been my contact and mentor, was promoted to the position of Vice President for the Middle East and relocated to the UAE. Despite the distance, maintained regular contact with him, valuing his guidance and support. However, he was eventually replaced by Another Gentleman, who had a strong bias against Indians.

Undeterred, I expressed my aspirations to him, hoping for a change in circumstances. He informed me that the Branch Manager position was typically reserved for German citizens, but it was not entirely impossible for individuals of other nationalities to attain it. He suggested that I undertake an internal study program and examination, with the requirement of achieving an impressive 80% mark. The catch, however, was that this program had to be completed in Germany, with a duration of three months.

This presented a significant challenge as it meant relocating to Germany for an extended period. Despite the obstacles, I decided to put my aspirations on hold for the time being, with the hope that circumstances might evolve in my favor. The path to achieving my career goals appeared to be a complex and challenging journey, but I remained determined to pursue my ambitions.

Another big move in my career came when Uwe visited Dammam the following month. We took a trip to Jubail in my car to meet with a customer, and during this journey, I once again expressed my intention to advance in my career. It was during this conversation that Uwe revealed his plan to transfer me to the Frankfurt airport office, filling in for a colleague who was going on maternity leave. His words felt like winning a multi-million-dollar lottery, and I was elated. He instructed me to prepare and train my successor in Dammam, making them capable of handling my responsibilities for three months.

During our conversation, Uwe had a phone discussion in German with Mr. Christ. Although I assumed it was a disagreement, I was pleasantly surprised when Uwe strongly supported my transfer.

Upon reaching Frankfurt, I found myself among colleagues I didn't previously know, and encountered bad approach against Indians at its peak in that office, with many of them was not treating me well. I enrolled in the free training course and, after completing my day's work, began my evening education. After two and a half months of rigorous training, the day of the examination arrived. There were 12 of us from different countries. Unfortunately, I failed the exam. I decided to give it another shot and improved my performance but was left with no further chances.

On that particular night, I received a call from Uwe, who was in Germany at the time. He sounded frustrated and even raised his voice during our conversation. It was clear that he was genuinely concerned about my situation. Despite his frustration, he didn't just go; he also proposed an alternative solution to the problem I was facing.

Thanks to his strong recommendation and advocacy on my behalf, my circumstances took a positive turn. As a result of his intervention, I was granted a rare and unexpected opportunity: a third chance to take the test. This was a significant lifeline, and I knew that it wouldn't have been possible without Uwe's support and influence.

The very next day, at around 9:30 AM German time, I seized the opportunity and retook the test. The pressure was high, but I was determined to make the most of this chance. It was a tense experience, but I knew it was my best shot at success.

Later that evening, I received an email from Mrs. Dancy Lane, presumably the person responsible for overseeing the test or making decisions about it. The email contained the news I had been eagerly awaiting: I had achieved the minimum score required to pass the test. I felt a rush of relief and gratitude wash over me.

While I was certainly grateful for the help and support, I had received from Uwe and Mrs. Dancy Lane, I couldn't ignore the fact that this success was almost entirely attributed to Uwe's strong recommendation. His advocacy and belief in me had been the driving force behind this positive outcome, and I couldn't have done it without him. This experience underscored the power of mentorship, support, and the impact that one person's recommendation can have on someone's life.

The following week, I flew back to Dammam and resumed my responsibilities. After just two months, I received the confirmation that had been waiting for - the assignment of Branch Manager. This journey was filled with challenges and unexpected twists, but it ultimately led to the realization of my career aspirations.

I believe in *POWER IS NOT GIVEN BUT TAKEN*, the strong intention to excel and advance in your career is the driving force that fuels continuous improvement. In-depth product knowledge allows for tailored solutions, and understanding the geography of your region, as well as the origin and destination of goods, is essential for efficient planning and execution. Combining these attributes with practical experience and a commitment to staying current in the field will undoubtedly help you reach new heights in your logistics career.

It appears that my tenure with this organization was relatively short-lived, lasting just a year following my promotion to Branch Manager. Unfortunately, during this time, tensions escalated between Christ and me, primarily stemming from disagreements over various branch-related matters, especially concerning sales activities and profitability. Despite our branch achieving an impressive 136% against budgeting targets, Christ was insistent on finding faults and initiating conflicts with my team members who had successfully met their targets.

I firmly believed in not allowing my team to be mistreated for trivial reasons and voiced my concerns to Uwe and European management. Regrettably, despite my efforts to address the situation, the issues persisted. Additionally, Christ brought in a personal acquaintance, Mr. Loy, who held a role as Regional Manager, further exacerbating the situation.

Given these circumstances, it became evident that it was time for me to step down from my position. This decision was driven by a commitment to maintaining a positive and respectful work environment for my team and myself, even if it meant relinquishing my role as Branch Manager.

When you find yourself in a workplace where the atmosphere has become toxic, and your relationship with management has soured, it's time to consider your options wisely. Your career is a significant part of your life, and it's vital to prioritize a work environment where you can thrive and contribute your best. Staying in such a situation for an extended period can lead to increased stress, decreased job satisfaction, and reduced productivity. The accumulation of this negative energy can hinder your professional growth and overall happiness. In these circumstances, it's often a wise decision to explore new job opportunities that align better with your goals and values. Don't be afraid to take that step toward a healthier, more supportive work environment where you can reach your full potential.

Planning a career transition is a significant step, and it's essential to adhere to certain policies and principles to ensure a smooth and ethical transition. While seeking new opportunities, it's crucial to have a firm offer from another company in place before making any changes. However, one critical rule in professional ethics is to never attempt to transfer any business or customer databases from your current employer to your prospective employer.

Such actions can be seen as untrustworthy and unethical, and they may raise concerns about your integrity and loyalty. It's essential to remember that the business relationships and customers you have built while working for a company belong to that organization, not to you personally. This principle is fundamental to maintaining professional ethics and integrity.

Without a solid foundation of ethics, any gains made during a transition can be tarnished, and your ability to be loyal to your own principles may be compromised. It's vital to uphold ethical standards throughout your career, as they are not only a reflection of your character but also a valuable asset in building trust and credibility in the professional world.

In my life, I've come to realize a profound lesson through a significant mistake made. Looking back, it's clear that the clash between my personal ego and professional uncertainties led me to make a decision without a solid backup plan, and this has proven to be the biggest mistake of my career.

What this experience taught me is that, as a logistician, you should always have not just a Plan B but also a Plan C ready, not just in terms of your career but in your daily work and strategies as well. The logistics field is ever-changing, and being adaptable and prepared for unforeseen challenges is paramount.

But the lesson doesn't end there but also realized the incredible importance of building relationships in our professional lives. It's not just about the people within your organization; it's about connecting with peers in similar industries and even your competitors. This network isn't just for the sake of networking; it's a source of support, collaboration, and inspiration. *NETWORK IS NET WORTH*

So, this made me to focus in building a professional circle that extended beyond the confines of my workplace. These connections with Managing Directors, Owners, and senior management from other logistics companies have enriched my industry knowledge and opened doors to exciting collaborations and opportunities. It's a testament to the enduring significance of adaptability, networking, and continuous learning in the dynamic world of logistics.

3

BECAME AN OWNER

In my life, there's been an unexplained force, whether you want to call it God or simply luck, that has often come to my aid when I've faced challenges and failed to find a Plan B. It's like a helping hand that appears just when I need it most, helping me overcome crises and navigate through difficult situations. This mysterious force has been a guiding presence, reminding me that even in the toughest times, there's often a way forward, and that with a bit of faith and perseverance, solutions can appear when we least expect them.

During the challenging period of my resignation with a 2-month notice period, my team members were understandably upset, and some tried to persuade me to reconsider my decision. Two of my colleagues even expressed their willingness to follow me, but I made a difficult choice to discourage them from taking that step. I didn't want my name to be associated with any potential disruptions or damages in the organization. It was my decision, and I didn't want others to make sacrifices on my behalf.

With my family in town, including my wife Sheeba and our first daughter Saptha, the situation was further complicated. I sent my family to Bahrain, where her family resides, which was a difficult but necessary move. I was left with a tight timeline of 60 days to find a new job; otherwise, I would have had to return home.

This is where the force of fate or luck, as previously mentioned, played a significant role in my life. I recalled a chance encounter with Mr. Hassan Al Nusef, a retired under-secretary to the Ministry of Commerce in Bahrain, during a plane journey a few years prior. During our conversation on that flight, he had shared his struggles with his small cargo and courier company, which was facing substantial losses. His words came back to me like a beacon of hope, and I promptly reached out to him, arranged a meeting in Manama, the capital of Bahrain, and we agreed to explore potential opportunities together.

The meeting with Mr. Hassan was exceptionally warm, and we explored two potential avenues for working together. The first option was to join his company as an employee, with a salary significantly lower than what I had at German company. The alternative was to take over the company under his sponsorship and run its operations. However, this option came with the condition of paying him a monthly royalty of 500 Bahraini Dinars.

Given the company's current financial state, it was impossible to commit to the royalty payment upfront. We reached an agreement that the royalty would commence once the company achieved breakeven status. Mr. Hassan Al Nusef offered his full support in dealing with banks and government organizations such as the seaport and airport authorities.

I opted for the second option, and the following day in Bahrain, we signed an agreement that marked the beginning of my journey as the owner of a logistics company. Challenges loomed large, I needed to inject initial capital and assemble an effective team. However, armed with my unwavering confidence as a salesperson, I decided to start as a one-man show, appointing staff as necessary. When you possess the mindset of a true salesperson, no challenge is too daunting to take on. I became the owner of **OEL**

My confidence as a salesperson was unwavering. I firmly believe that a true salesperson possesses the skill and strategy to sell any product in any market. To me, the essence of meeting a customer isn't about discussing business upfront. My strong belief, based on years of experience, is that these meetings serve to build relationships and establish a bond between the customer and service provider.

My approach was distinct, and always set up appointments with customers beforehand, focusing on personal conversations and updates about their business. During these encounters, I never pushed rates or tried to make a sale on the spot. Instead, aimed to understand their requirements fully. If it is need are can be accomplished, then made a commitment to work as a consultant, supporting their specific demands.

I've never been a proponent of selling at the lowest price. In my view, we have the right to sell our products at our suggested prices. Selling solely based on the lowest price diminishes the role of a salesperson and reduces it to a simple transaction. I've always strived to avoid being seen as a cheap salesperson.

Sales and marketing are indeed an art form that hinges on understanding customer needs and delivering accordingly. Extensive homework is vital in this process. Learning about the customer, their products, management, trade lines, and clients is essential. This knowledge allows you to tailor your approach to each customer, applying a winning strategy. Without thorough research, a salesperson is likely to face challenges. Additionally, evaluating the personality and attitude of your contact in the customer's office plays a crucial role in the process. Sales is a multi-step journey, and the quality of a successful salesperson depends on their probing ability to uncover and meet the unique needs of each customer.

Arriving in Bahrain, often referred to as the "City of Pearls," I felt a unique sense of freedom and openness that contrasted with Saudi Arabia. The culture and lifestyle here were more adaptable to my preferences. My primary mission was to translate the well-thought-out plan I had drafted during my transition in Saudi Arabia into practical and actionable strategies.

In any business, whether it's in services or products, there are benchmarks that require deep knowledge. This includes understanding your competitors, the market conditions, and the political stability of the region.

A draft policy and strategies were developed to execute over the first three months and then adjusted them for the next nine months to a year. Based on this, I conducted budgeting and evaluated revenue and profitability expectations.

Starting a new company from the ground up necessitates careful preparation. You must engage in strategic planning to identify potential customers and set rough budgeting targets for each customer. This process demands a deep understanding of the customer's requirements and the countries from which they import. Building strong relationships with agents in specific regions is crucial, focusing on sales to establish your presence in the market. Although I personally prefer not to sell at lower rates, for a quick penetration of the local market, adopting this approach for a short period can be effective. This could be recommended for an initial 3-6 month.

During that time, approximately 80% of customers were importing goods from China. For the first six months, my concentration was on this trade route, making multiple visits to China to meet with various agents and establish personal connections that would make it hard for them to overlook me. Initially, and sold containers at cost, and within three months, we had booked 22 containers with four customers. However, my total profit was less than $500, which wasn't even enough to cover the building rent. Nevertheless, I managed to gain the confidence and support of 25 loyal customers within a year, most of whom were revenue-sharing businesses. I must admit that I didn't adhere strictly to ethics during this period, as my strong desire was to succeed and achieve my second-year goals. During this phase, we hired six new employees: four in sales, one in operations, and one as a messenger. Previously, I had handled all of these responsibilities myself.

My advice to new investors in the logistics industry is to avoid jumping in without proper planning or merely relying on someone else's encouragement. It's crucial to have a thorough understanding of the market, processes, and procedures, even more so than your subordinates. This way, you can step in and take charge if someone is absent or sick, serving as a role model to your team.

As part of our OEL branding efforts, we placed a strong emphasis on building social acquaintances and fostering personal relationships. We went beyond traditional business interactions and engaged with our customers on a more personal level. This included visiting our customers' families, inviting them to dinners, organizing outings, and celebrating special occasions together.

We made sure to acknowledge and respect the diverse cultural and religious backgrounds of our customers. We organized events such as iftar during Ramadan, Christmas celebrations, and Onam festivities. These initiatives helped us connect with our customers on a deeper level and create a sense of camaraderie.

Our approach to sales was not limited to a single strategy but rather multifaceted. We believed in giving our sales team a considerable degree of freedom while adhering to our organizational policies and individual target. This approach empowered our salespeople to customize their strategies according to the specific needs and preferences of each customer. Consequently, it not only strengthened our relationships with customers but also amplified our brand presence in the industry."

I take great pride in acknowledging that the rapid growth of my company was not solely the result of my efforts but, more significantly, the collective effort of my dedicated team. Over the course of three years, OEL had the privilege of working with 22 exceptionally talented team members, each contributing their unique skills and expertise to our shared success.

In the logistics industry, employees can often be categorized into three distinct groups:

1. **Wish to Happen:** These employees tend to be passive and wait for things to happen. They may lack motivation or the drive to take initiative in their work. They often rely on external factors or luck to bring about results.

2. **Let it Happen:** This group represents employees who are somewhat proactive but not fully committed to making things happen. They may take action when necessary but might not go the extra mile to ensure success. They tend to follow the status quo and are less inclined to take risks.

3. **Make it Happen:** These are the proactive and highly motivated individuals who take charge of their responsibilities. They are driven, ambitious, and determined to achieve their goals. They actively seek opportunities and are not afraid to take calculated risks to make things happen. They are often the most valuable contributors to the organization.

In the dynamic field of logistics, having employees who fall into the "Make it Happen" category is crucial for success. These individuals are more likely to drive innovation, overcome challenges, and contribute significantly to the company's growth. However, it's also important to nurture and develop employees from the other categories to unlock their potential and foster a culture of continuous improvement.

In our organization, the criteria for talent acquisition extended beyond just product knowledge. Out of the 22 individuals on our team, 20 were selected primarily for their aggressive attitude, determination, and eagerness to explore new product areas. Equally important was their recognition of the significance of employment and financial needs.

We adopted a strategy of training and shaping fresh talent to align with our organizational and market requirements. Our approach was to provide individuals with the autonomy to foster their growth, both personally and within the organization. This philosophy of nurturing talent while allowing for individual and organizational development proved to be highly effective and contributed significantly to our success.

I firmly believe in the principle of avoiding micromanagement and not attempting to oversee every detail of the business. In an industry as dynamic and multifaceted as logistics, micromanagement can be counterproductive. Instead, it's essential to foster an environment where employees are encouraged to take personal ownership of their roles and responsibilities.

In the logistics field, it's crucial for team members to feel a sense of ownership and commitment to the organization's success. They should perceive the company as their own and be motivated to contribute to its growth and prosperity. In this context, a well-structured hierarchy management system is more powerful and effective than a micromanagement approach. It allows employees to have a clear understanding of their roles, responsibilities, and areas of influence within the organization while providing the freedom to innovate and excel in their respective domains. This approach not only promotes a healthier work culture but also leads to enhanced productivity and job satisfaction among team members.

In the dynamic world of logistics, where every movement counts, my journey with OEL has been a tale of remarkable experiences that have fueled my confidence and determination. There's a saying that goes, "Sometimes, you need to think outside the box to seize opportunities," and one such extraordinary opportunity came our way as Alba (Aluminum Bahrain). The biggest Aluminum smelters in the world

The genesis of this unforgettable journey began when Mr. Hassan Al Nusef shared the information that Alba was planning a colossal move: the transportation of a transformer from Mitsubishi Electrical to their facility. While other trading company of Hassan was on Alba's vendor list, OEL was not. The mission was to move 175 metric tons of machinery, measuring a whopping 365 cubic meters. The odds were stacked against us from the outset, but I was determined to rise to the challenge.

The first hurdle we faced was not being on the vendor list, making us ineligible to attend the tender. However, our unwavering commitment to this mega project led us down a different path. We managed to obtain the tender documents through Mr. Al Nusef's other company, setting the stage for an audacious journey ahead.

The road ahead was fraught with challenges. We needed to find a seasoned agent in Japan, secure a suitable break bulk ship equipped with a crane, create meticulous loading and unloading charts, plan the transportation route, and navigate the intricate web of traffic permissions. These were just the tip of the iceberg, but my prior experience with SAFCO's mega moves had provided a foundation. Financial security and fund was another problem along with the other issues, I was poised to shoulder all responsibilities, including potential losses, with unwavering resolve.

Amidst a sea of competitors, Atlantic Forwarding Group offered an enticing rate that could secure us this project. With a minimal profit margin of just 60K, we submitted our proposal through Mr. Al Nusef's other company. After rigorous evaluations, both our technical and financial proposals received approval, and Hassan signed the agreement with Alba. The scope of work was nothing short of daunting, from the ex-works pickup in Tokyo to the final placement on Alba's platform, including jack and jerk offloading.

With approval in hand, we found ourselves standing on the precipice of financial strain. Our company's coffers held a mere 50,000 BHD, far from sufficient for the mammoth task at hand. Using my belief that "every lock has a key" as my guiding principle, I embarked on a journey to Japan to meet Mr. Garry, the owner of Atlantic Forwarding Group. His previous visits to Bahrain, where he shared moments with my family, had cultivated a personal connection that eased the path to presenting the stark reality of the colossal financial involvement required for this undertaking.

The success of our undertaking hinged on transparency, a principle I held in high regard. When I met with Mr. Garry, I didn't shy away from revealing the complete cost sheet, which starkly showcased our profit margin of 60K. In this complex dealing, I made it crystal clear that any profits or losses incurred would be distributed evenly among all parties involved.

However, a moment of discretion prevailed in my dealings with Hassan. I chose not to disclose the full cost sheet to him. The rationale behind this decision stemmed from the fact that Hassan was not a business partner in the traditional sense; he was an official sponsor. Drawing from my experiences in the Middle East, where business dynamics often differ from the norm, I believed it was prudent to withhold certain financial details from him. This decision was guided by a desire to maintain the integrity of our partnership while aligning with the customary practices I had encountered in that region.

A breakthrough came when Mr. Garry generously extended 45 days of credit, covering 80% of the project's total cost. The remaining local charges would be managed by Hassan, who expressed his commitment to seeing our venture succeed. This collaborative spirit was a testament to the idea that there's always a force supporting us when we truly need it.

Over the next 67 days, our team worked tirelessly, following a meticulously planned schedule and checking off daily tasks. Numerous unexpected challenges arose, and there were moments when it seemed like we might lose the entire project. However, our unwavering determination, multi-level approach, and persuasive skills helped us surmount every obstacle.

In the end, against all odds, we emerged victorious. The transformer was successfully transported, placed on Alba's platform, and the project was completed. This journey had tested our mettle, but it had also solidified our belief in the power of determination, collaboration, and thinking outside the box. It was a reminder that in the world of logistics, ***every challenge is an opportunity*** waiting to be seized, and with the right approach, even the most complex projects can be conquered.

Drawing from my own experience and as a piece of advice, I would strongly recommend that, in the world of logistics, taking ownership of your decisions and actions is a cornerstone of success. In this field, we are not infallible, and there will be times when despite our best efforts, we encounter setbacks and challenges. However, these moments are not indicative of failure but rather opportunities for growth and learning. It's crucial to remember that while you may not win every time or accumulate wealth with every endeavor, the knowledge gained from each experience is invaluable. The resilience and determination you exhibit in the face of adversity will ultimately define your career and personal growth. So, embrace every challenge as a chance to improve, and celebrate the days when your hard work and tenacity lead to success.

4

GROWTH ADDITION

Worldwide Express, an international courier service brand operating independently in various countries, brought forth a valuable lesson – that proving one's capability to handle diverse tasks often opens doors to new opportunities. In Bahrain, where Mr. Hassa was managing the branch progress had not been steady but lacked significant improvement.

One memorable chapter in this journey unfolded during a trip to Qatar with Hassan, which happened to be just a week after the birth of my second daughter, Sarga. My typical role did not involve direct participation in WWE day-to-day activities. However, on this occasion, Hassan requested that I create a presentation and a comprehensive business plan for an upcoming conference. Despite my primary background in logistics and limited knowledge of the courier industry, I took up the challenge. Drawing from my logistical experience and recognizing the similarities between both industries in terms of efficiency and attention to detail, I crafted a presentation that met the task at hand. I presented the same in conference and many people agreed with my thought process.

Upon our return from Qatar, a pivotal moment occurred. Hassan visited my office, and in a candid conversation, he expressed his intention for me to assume control of WWL in Bahrain. His belief in my ability to effectively manage and develop the branch was a significant vote of confidence. We delved into the financial aspects, royalty agreements, and the transition of responsibilities. In the end, we reached a mutual agreement, and I took the helm of the company.

Through this experience, I came to firmly believe that opportunities are akin to the goddess Lakshmi. She seldom graces us with her presence, and not everyone recognizes her arrival or knows how to welcome her. It's not merely about working hard; it's about working smarter. When opportunity does knock, it's crucial not only to seize it but also to maximize its potential. The true power of an opportunity often lies in its capacity to spawn further opportunities, provided it is embraced and harnessed skillfully.

In retrospect, my journey with WWL in Bahrain serves as a testament to the idea that demonstrating your capabilities and being open to new challenges can lead to transformative opportunities. It underscores the importance of recognizing these opportunities when they arise and having the courage and vision to accept them, even when they may lie outside your immediate area of expertise. Each opportunity seized becomes a steppingstone toward realizing your full potential and achieving success.

OEL had a significant presence in the region, with branch offices not only in Bahrain but also in Dubai, and another three additional offices in Saudi Arabia. The collective workforce of these offices totalled 65 dedicated professionals.

One of the key strengths of OEL's operations was the facilitation of cross-trade shipments and Less than Container Load (LCL) shipments via the strategic locations of Bahrain and Dubai. These services allowed the company to tap into the growing demand for international trade and shipping solutions in the region.

The ability to efficiently handle cross-trade shipments and LCL cargo was a testament to OEL's logistical expertise and its commitment to providing comprehensive solutions to its clients. We were de-consolidating almost 25-30 LCL boxes average in month. This diverse and dynamic range of services likely contributed significantly to the company's reputation and success in the logistics industry during this time.

In WWL, even though we've onboarded numerous new contractual clients, I must admit that I haven't achieved the level of success I had hoped for. There are a variety of factors at play here, one of which is my primary focus on OEL I've made attempts to invigorate express business by bringing in fresh sales talents, but I've come to a sobering realization about my own shortcomings in this endeavor.

Looking back, I see that I failed to conduct the necessary groundwork and feasibility study before taking on the responsibility of WLL. Bahrain, a small island nation, boasts the presence of industry giants. Competing and sustaining a presence in such a challenging market was no small feat. It's clear to me now that I allowed myself to become complacent when opportunity knocked, neglecting the crucial step of conducting thorough research and analysis.

Furthermore, my intense focus on courier business led to a significant deviation from my core expertise in logistics, which has long been the bedrock of my career. In hindsight, this shift was a warning sign I should have heeded. While diversification is a valid business strategy, it must be pursued with utmost diligence and commitment to ensure that each venture receives the attention it deserves.

This chapter in my journey has underscored the importance of striking a balance between exploration and consolidation. While seizing new opportunities is vital, it's equally essential to maintain a deep understanding of the markets and industries in which we operate. Going forward, I'm committed to approaching new ventures with a more discerning eye, a dedication to thorough research, and a renewed focus on my core expertise in logistics.

the Courier business was facing really tough for us while competing with giants. However, the Salesperson within me refused to give up and was determined to uncover new opportunities through my network of friends. That's when Sheikh Ali Al Khalifa, the son of Shaik Muhammed Al Khalifa (who served as the transport minister and later as the Minister of Ports and Customs), introduced me to the Vice President of Ahli United Bank. This individual was responsible for overseeing the delivery of credit/debit cards, EWA bills, and more.

For many days, we engaged in discussions with him, often in the company of Shaik Ali. Finally, proposal was submitted with a revolutionary idea - the Ahli United Bank Post Office System. Until that point, the bank had been relying on its own staff, offering them high salaries and various benefits including vehicles, but the system was proving to be ineffective and burdensome.

My proposal aimed to change this potential service laps. We wouldn't use the bank's staff or vehicles. Instead, we'd make use of a small area in their office space located in the basement. This wasn't solely my idea; it was the brainchild of my friend who had previously worked at United Parcel Service (UPS). With this new proposal, the bank would benefit from efficient delivery services without interruptions. If any staff member was on leave, we had a reliable backup plan in place.

Truth be told, it wasn't the most profitable venture. Sometimes, you need to pursue businesses that enhance your reputation within the industry, even if immediate profitability isn't guaranteed. This was a fundamental policy I adhered to - look beyond short-term gains and focus on long-term potential. Finding such opportunities is challenging, but it's essential to try. In fact, I heard this from most of the business experts that not to entertain or engage in business where you cannot find better profitability.

In this instance, I didn't give up on courier business. Alongside my logistics business, I continued to explore new doors and opportunities. Surprisingly, the less profitable venture eventually led me to become a part of the government postal service for a period of 10 months during a period of political upheaval in Bahrain. During this time, I managed to generate unexpected profits, demonstrating the value of perseverance and adaptability in the world of business, even in challenging and uncertain times.

During a period of political unrest, a faction of our country's population rose against the ruling party and family, gaining control over key government institutions like the Health Ministry and Postal Department. This tumultuous time saw many government institutions shuttered, with the military assuming control to maintain law and order. The streets became a battleground, barricaded by the armed forces of both Saudi Arabia and Bahrain to quell the protests and violence.

In the midst of this chaos, a pivotal moment occurred when I received a call directed by Mr. Hassan Al Nusef, the official sponsor of our company. The call came from the Department of Postal Service within the Ministry of Transportation, urgently requesting a meeting with Hassan and me. Navigating the heavily fortified streets, we arrived on time for the meeting. The area was teeming with both military and police personnel, but with the unexpected help of a security guard from the Postal Department, we were granted access. We were ushered into a large conference hall and served with a special black tea.

After a brief wait, a group of individuals entered the room, including Shaikh Muhammed al Khalifa, Khalifa (the father of my friend Shaikh Ali), and a team of 14 people, which included the undersecretary of the Postal Department, Shaikh Bader. Without much ceremony, they began to explain the gravity of the situation, emphasizing the need for strict confidentiality. They informed us that all postal delivery staff had gone on strike, resulting in a significant backlog of critical consignments, including court notices, credit and debit cards, bank statements, and registered mail. They expressed reluctance to involve major courier companies or others due to concerns about potential anti-government involvement among their staff, fearing that the project could be compromised.

The challenge before us was daunting. We needed to not only sort through this mountain of mail but also navigate the complex logistics of delivering it in a politically charged and protest-ridden environment. The government pledged its support, allocating 15 rental cars for our use and tasking us with commencing deliveries the very next day. Sorting based on specific blocks and roads mentioned in the addresses added to the complexity of the task. Moreover, we faced a severe shortage of manpower, and with most areas under the control of protesters, recruiting additional help on short notice proved almost impossible.

We embarked on a journey to tackle this enormous undertaking, seeking assistance from our team members and connections within our social circles. A friend in the police department pledged to provide support in the evenings, while housewives, including my own wife and the wives of our staff, joined forces to assist in sorting. This collective effort involved nearly 60 people, including a team responsible for newspaper delivery, all engaged in this herculean task. Despite our best efforts, we fell short, achieving only a 60% completion rate.

Each morning, I found myself attending meetings at the Ministry with Shaikh Bader, providing updates on the delivery status and highlighting pending issues. It became evident that our failure stemmed from our initial approach of assigning equal priority to all deliveries. We then shifted our strategy, focusing on prioritizing the delivery of registered post and court notices, which proved to be the right approach.

The project continued for a gruelling six months. As time passed, the local issues subsided, with the military successfully restoring order and normalcy. As the project came to a close, we submitted our invoice, and to our astonishment, the Ministry approved a bill that exceeded our expectations.

This experience taught me a profound lesson that I am eager to share with others. It underscored the importance of identifying the unique demands and requirements of a situation, sometimes placing profitability on the back burner. By responding to those demands with exceptional performance and service, one can achieve remarkable success. Transparency and integrity in all dealings are vital, as they ultimately lead to success. My story serves as a testament to the power of adaptability, collaboration, prioritization, resourcefulness, and dedication to delivering exceptional service, even in the face of the most

In the ever-evolving landscape of business and logistics, one fundamental truth stands out – there is no permanent, foolproof strategy. Markets, technologies, and customer demands shift continuously, demanding adaptability from those in charge. A logistician's most valuable quality lies in their capacity to gracefully compromise with their strategy, aligning it with the ever-changing requirements and demands of the situation. Hurdles are inevitable, but a skilled logistician excels at easing these roadblocks, finding creative solutions to keep the supply chain flowing. Moreover, there's wisdom in engaging in productive discussions, even with your customers, when a strategy isn't yielding the expected results. Instead, the focus should be on internal problem-solving and swift adjustments, ensuring that the business remains agile and ready to pivot as circumstances dictate.

Going back to the OEL business, the global recession of 2008-2009 left an indelible mark on our organization, and it was a trying period that tested our financial fortitude. At the heart of the turmoil was a considerable setback - many of our valued customers, including our main client, were understandably cautious about settling their invoices. This hesitancy created a domino effect within our financial ecosystem. Payables began to accumulate at an alarming rate, and the relentless pressure from our vendors only added to our mounting concerns. Our financial stability teetered precariously on the edge of a precipice.

In response to this dire situation, I felt compelled to explore options for securing additional financing. I discussed this matter with my colleague, Hassan, though his apparent reluctance to engage with the bank added another layer of complexity to an already challenging scenario.

Despite the turbulent circumstances, we ultimately managed to navigate our way through the storm. It was during this period that I made a pivotal decision – I chose not to repatriate funds from our operations in India to alleviate the financial pressure we were facing. Looking back, it was a decision driven by prudence, and it proved to be a shrewd one.

Reflecting on this experience, I believe it offers a valuable lesson to the readers. In times of financial hardship and adversity, it's crucial to resist the impulse to transfer funds from your home country to mitigate problems. Instead, it's often more prudent to confront the hurdles with the resources and facilities you have at your disposal. Attempting to repatriate funds under duress can frequently exacerbate the challenges you face and may, in fact, signify a failure to address the core issues effectively. By facing adversity head-on and leveraging the tools available within your current framework, you're more likely to emerge from such trials stronger and better equipped for the future.

In the dynamic landscape of the Middle East, every endeavour and every shipment presents a unique learning opportunity. It's a region where experience is not just valued; it's an invaluable teacher. Each day brings forth fresh challenges, and in the world of logistics and business, these challenges often demand innovative solutions.

One crucial lesson is not merely to follow someone else's instructions when facing issues, but to dig deeper and truly understand the root of the problem. This requires a careful and analytical approach. Instead of relying solely on preconceived solutions, it's essential to engage with the issue at hand, dissect it, and ascertain its underlying causes.

In the pursuit of resolution, seeking advice from experts is a prudent strategy. Experts can offer insights and perspectives that may not be immediately apparent. They can provide guidance that is grounded in their wealth of experience, helping you navigate complex situations with greater ease and confidence.

In essence, the Middle East teaches us that adaptability, a thirst for knowledge, and the wisdom to seek expert advice are not just virtues but essential tools for success in this ever-evolving and challenging region.

In the aftermath of the recession, my professional relationship with Hassan took an unexpected turn. During the crucial moments of signing audit reports, he began to pose numerous questions and eagerly voiced his opinions on the audit findings. The tension in the room was palpable as his inquiries seemed to challenge the established norms of our collaboration.

Furthermore, Hassan broached the topic of sponsorship fees, seeking an increase in financial support from our organization. After careful consideration and deliberation, I made the decision to agree to his request, recognizing the importance of maintaining a harmonious working relationship in these post-recession times.

5

BREAKUP

In between, Mr. Hassan requested me to accommodate his son, Hamad, who had recently returned from the United States after completing his MBA in finance. Hamad was eager to gain some hands-on experience in the local market before venturing into a career with a bank or a financial corporation. It seemed like a mutually beneficial arrangement, so I arranged a place for him in our accounts department.

Little did I know that this seemingly innocuous decision would evolve into one of the most significant threat I'd face in my professional life. As Hamad settled into his role, a series of events began to unfold, altering the dynamics within the organization in unexpected ways.

The situation escalated as Hamad began to question established practices and proposed alternative strategies that didn't always align with my long-standing principles. These differences in vision led to internal conflicts and created a sense of instability within the organization. I have corrected him many times and warned not to take any decision without my approval and same has informed to Hassan.

I used to travel a lot as a part of business development. And in one such travel, Hamad migrated to my cabin and placed his table in my executive office, after my travel I noticed this and removed the same and expelled him from organization. Hassan did not respond to this for a week or two.

On a seemingly ordinary Wednesday morning, Hassan Al Nusef entered my office with a declaration that would send shockwaves through our relationship. He asserted that everything I had done was on his son was not good, boldly claiming that he was the rightful owner of our organization, OEL. I was taken aback by his audacious statement and immediately attempted to clarify the situation, providing a detailed account of the company's history and my contributions. However, Hassan remained steadfast in his conviction, unwilling to acknowledge the facts as they stood.

In a surprising turn of events, he proposed a separation of our collaboration. He approached the matter with politeness and suggested that we undertake the process of asset allocation and auditing as a first step of separation. This proposition set off alarm bells in my mind, as I sensed the gravity of the situation. Nevertheless, I decided to engage in a dialogue and, against my better judgment, agreed to a 50-50 agreement. This agreement was particularly unsettling since I knew, without a doubt, that I had contributed 100% to the company's success.

This decision was not taken lightly, and it weighed heavily on my conscience. It felt like a compromise forced upon me, a bitter pill to swallow in the face of a situation that seemed to be spiralling out of control. As I contemplated the path ahead, I couldn't help but wonder how I had arrived at this juncture and what lay in store for me in the uncertain chapters that awaited.

After much deliberation, the discussions concluded with an agreement to part ways on a 50-50 basis, a decision that had weighed heavily on me. However, it soon became apparent that this separation was not going to be a straightforward process. Hassan introduced a new twist to the arrangement – I was to be solely responsible for collecting all the outstanding receivables to compensate for my share of the company. Additionally, I was tasked with managing the payables.

This arrangement posed a considerable challenge. In the wake of the ongoing issues at OEL and the news of our impending separation, it was evident that collecting outstanding payments from customers would be an uphill battle. Clients were hesitant to settle their dues, and it seemed that we would need to exert significant effort to convince vendors to extend patience as we navigated this transitional period.

The situation felt like a complex chess match, with each move carefully calculated to safeguard our respective interests. While the decision to part ways had been reached, the practical implementation of this agreement presented a myriad of obstacles.

It was a test of determination, negotiation skills, and resilience as I ventured into the turbulent waters of managing receivables and payables, striving to ensure a fair and equitable resolution to our business relationship.

In the face of daunting challenges, I embarked on a mission to resolve the financial issues stemming from our separation agreement. Armed with determination and a deep understanding of my customers, I embarked on a journey to meet each one personally, impressing upon them the gravity of our situation. It was a testament to the relationships I had built over the years, as 98% of these customers agreed to pay their dues promptly.

Similarly, I extended my efforts to reach out to vendors, traversing the regions both within and outside of the GCC. With careful persuasion and well-honed negotiation skills, I managed to convince them to be patient and flexible during this transitional phase.

This experience underscores the essence of a logistician's role in navigating complex challenges. It serves as a shining example of the logistician's capacity for negotiation and customer persuasion, traits that are essential in the world of logistics and supply chain management. A logistician often encounters numerous hurdles in the course of their career, but the key is never to give up. Instead, it's about finding creative and effective solutions through crisis management, a skill that can prove invaluable in various aspects of logistics, including the timely delivery of goods and handling unforeseen challenges. It's a testament to the resilience and adaptability that define the core qualities of a logistician.

The resolution of our business separation took an unexpected and, in my view, unethical turn. I was offered a mere BHD 30,000 as a settlement, a proposition that I firmly declined. In a surprising twist, Hassan took possession of all the company's assets and retained our customer base.

It was a deeply disheartening turn of events, and it felt like a chapter in my life was closing in an unjust and disloyal manner. Throughout this ordeal, I couldn't help but sense the presence of some supernatural force at play, as if the very forces of destiny were supported me.

In an unexpected twist, Hassan proposed that I continue with the organization, albeit in a different capacity – as an employee. This decision required me to set aside my ego, frustrations, and pride. Despite the injustice I felt, I chose to accept this offer, recognizing the need for time to recover from the shock and to rebuild my resilience.

This transitional period also allowed me the space and time to strategize for the future. I knew that I needed to formulate a new and robust plan, one that would not only help me overcome the setbacks but also pave the way for a brighter and more promising tomorrow. It was a pivotal moment in my journey, marked by resilience, adaptability, and an unwavering determination to rise above the challenges that life had thrown my way.

The turn of events that followed Hassan's sale of the company to a Saudi-based group was disheartening and challenging, marked by unprofessional conduct and ill-treatment directed towards me. It was during this trying period that I had the privilege of meeting Mr. Thomas, the Managing Director of the Japanese logistics giant and subsidiary of Japanese Railways, a professional and trusted friend.

Over the course of nearly a month, Mr. Thomas and I engaged in extensive discussions, sharing our visions and aspirations. It became evident that the Kingdom of Bahrain held immense potential for his company, and we saw an opportunity to establish a thriving logistics enterprise in the region. For me it was a golden opportunity to revenge Hassan and new owners.

The aftermath of my resignation from this company unfolded into a protracted legal battle, marked by unsettling and distressing events. When I submitted my resignation and requested the cancellation of my visa, they retained my passport, a clear violation of the law. In response, I sought legal counsel, and based on my lawyer's advice, I filed a lawsuit against the organization. The act of withholding an Indian passport is a criminal offense, as it is the property of the Indian government, and individuals are merely its custodians.

In an effort to regain possession of my passport, I obtained an emergency execution order, which compelled the company to return it. However, this move triggered a retaliatory response from them. They filed both a criminal and civil case against me, seeking a substantial sum of 45,000 BHD.

The consequences of these legal actions were far-reaching. As the criminal case proceeded, I found myself placed under a travel ban, unable to leave the country. Simultaneously, my bank accounts were frozen, exacerbating the financial strain on me and my family.

The most distressing development came when officers from the Criminal Investigation Department (CID) visited my home, requesting my presence at the public prosecutor's office. This experience was emotionally taxing and deeply unsettling for both me and my family.

The situation took a toll on my personal life as well. OEL seized my car, forcing me to rely on public transportation, an unfamiliar and inconvenient adjustment in the Kingdom. The ordeal placed immense stress on my family, and their suffering weighed heavily on my shoulders.

This chapter in my life serves as a stark reminder of the complexities and challenges that can arise when legal disputes escalate, especially in a foreign country. It underscores the importance of legal counsel, resilience in the face of adversity, and the unwavering pursuit of justice.

In the challenging period when my passport was wrongfully held by the company, I took a decisive step to safeguard my interests and continue my professional journey. I entrusted all the necessary updates and documentation to my trusted friend, Thomas, who had been a steadfast companion throughout this ordeal. With my documents securely in his possession, I made the bold move to join with Thomas as their first employee in the Kingdom of Bahrain.

My role as a county Manager with responsibility of MD of Bahrain involved the daunting task of establishing offices, obtaining licenses, and securing the necessary approvals. It was a time of intense dedication and hard work as we worked tirelessly to lay the foundation for a thriving logistics operation in the region.

The freezing of my bank account created a financial hurdle, but Thomas came to my aid. He managed to convince the management to deposit my salary into his European account and provided me with cash support, which was an invaluable lifeline during this period.

In parallel, I pursued every avenue to regain control of my personal and professional life. I obtained special permission from the court to procure a duplicate passport, a critical step towards reclaiming my freedom. With the new passport in hand and the unwavering support of my colleagues, I successfully had my visa stamped, allowing me to move forward with renewed hope and determination.

This phase of my journey exemplifies the resilience and resourcefulness required to navigate complex and unforeseen challenges. It underscores the significance of unwavering friendships and the importance of taking bold steps when faced with adversity. Above all, it speaks to the indomitable spirit that propels us forward even in the face of seemingly insurmountable obstacles.

6

REVENGE

Even though I had achieved financial stability that spanned for two generations, my decision to continue working in the region, particularly with the new Japan logistics giant, was driven by one compelling reason: a burning desire for professional revenge against Hassan and his new partners. This motivation was so powerful that it overshadowed all other considerations.

I was resolute in my determination to develop this company's presence in Bahrain and to regain all the customers I had diligently secured during my time with my own previous office. It was a decision that sometimes conflicted with my personal ethics, but the need for professional vindication was paramount in my mind.

The complexity of this situation is a testament to the intricate balance between personal values, professional ambitions, and the pursuit of justice. It demonstrates the moral dilemmas that can arise in the professional world and the sacrifices that individuals are willing to make to achieve their goals. In my case, it reflects my unwavering determination to right what I perceived as a professional wrong and to succeed in the face of adversity, no matter the cost.

In my quest to execute my policy of professional revenge, my initial strategy was to reassemble my old team members who had performed exceptionally well during my tenure at OEL. It was clear that the new management lacked the necessary experience and expertise in the logistics industry. This deficiency often led to conflicts within the team, eroding their confidence in effectively managing sales. To make matters worse, the sales incentives that had previously motivated the team were abruptly halted.

My former team members, feeling the impact of these changes, approached me for guidance. However, I decided not to join them with me at that moment, as I was acutely aware of the potential consequences for both my personal and professional reputation. Being perceived as a betrayer in the market was a risk I was unwilling to take.

Instead, I patiently and discreetly orchestrated a series of moves. One by one, I pulled my former team members into new setup, offering them positions that honoured their skills and experiences, along with competitive wages. This strategic move had a profound impact. Once we joined forces at here, our collective efforts paid off, resulting in the addition of a significant number of customers to the company's roster.

Absolutely, as a professional in a senior leadership role, it is crucial to recognize the potential strengths of your team and plan effectively without disrupting the market. This story highlights the importance of collaboration and the remarkable resilience of a well-coordinated team. It serves as a powerful example that even in challenging situations, strategic decision-making and a steadfast commitment to excellence can pave the way for remarkable successes.

After enduring a gruelling 10-month legal battle, the lower court delivered a verdict that deemed me not guilty, leading to the dissolution of my legal indemnity and official benefits. Simultaneously, my travel ban and bank account freeze were lifted, providing some relief.

However, the opposition did not relent and decided to appeal the decision, taking the case to the middle court. To my relief, I emerged victorious once again, securing a compensation of 34,000 BHD. Despite the overwhelming evidence against them, they persisted in their efforts to disrupt my life and create turmoil.

Their persistence led to the case being elevated to the upper court, even though they were fully aware that the evidence was stacked against them. Remarkably, the upper court reached the same conclusion after a year of deliberation and warned the opposing team against further harassment.

On a separate legal front, I had filed a case to retain possession of my passport. In a significant turn of events, the manager of owner was sentenced to two months of detention in connection with this case.

This legal journey has been arduous and filled with challenges, but it also underscores the importance of perseverance and a commitment to upholding one's rights in the face of adversity.

For anyone contemplating investments in the Middle East, it's essential to maintain a disciplined approach when it comes to documentation and legal support. Over my years of experience, I've learned that in the intricate world of business relationships, you can never predict when a partnership might sour, and your once-trusted partners may become adversaries. That's why I strongly emphasize the need for vigilance. Ensuring that you have a well-documented and legally solid framework in place is not just a smart move; it's a necessity. This advice is born from personal experience and is a reminder to all prospective investors that being proactive in safeguarding your interests is paramount, especially in the ever-evolving landscape of international business.

My relationship with Thomas was characterized by a professional demeanor in the office, but it took on a very personal tone outside of work. When it came to business matters, our interactions were marked by intense and robust discussions. We engaged in substantial arguments, but they were always in a healthy and constructive manner. During the early stages of our joint discussions, company emphasized a few key objectives as the mandatory targets.

Securing business from a Japanese electrical company in Middle East was a significant priority and target for me. This Japanese electrical giant had been a coveted target for some time, and our success in winning their business was a game-changer. The company HQ had previously attempted to establish business entry with them directly from Japan, but their efforts had been thwarted by a peculiar twist of fate. It turned out that there were personal conflicts between our company's staff in Tokyo and the logistics head at our client in Japan, who happened to be an ex-husband and ex-wife. This personal history had created an unexpected barrier to their business endeavors, and it opened up a unique opportunity for us to bridge the gap and secure their business in the Middle East.

Within a remarkably short span of six months, I managed to establish strong connections with several individuals in their logistics department. These relationships proved instrumental in generating some initial inquiries on a case-by-case basis. While these inquiries were not our ultimate target, they were a crucial step towards becoming a registered vendor for them and engaging in contractual business with them.

I was well aware of the formidable challenge we faced, considering that we were going head-to-head with other major competitor in freight forwarding industry, a major player handling the lion's share of customers logistics business. Nonetheless, the groundwork we had laid and the relationships we had nurtured were promising signs of progress in our pursuit of this coveted partnership.

A year later, the Japanese customer demanded us to participate in the ISO certification process, which served as a preliminary step towards vendor registration. This marked a significant milestone in our journey with my target customer, and it was a clear sign of their growing trust in our capabilities. As time progressed, we were gradually invited to handle more substantial shipments and tackle increasingly complex logistics challenges.

Just a month after obtaining our ISO certificate, we received the coveted invitation to formally submit our application for vendor registration. This was the culmination of several intricate procedures, inspections, and evaluations that we had undergone to meet their stringent standards. Upon gaining approval, we eagerly submitted our first tender documents, complete with a comprehensive price structure covering various regions from the Middle East to Africa.

For me and organization, this was a momentous occasion, and it brought our entire senior management team from the Netherlands regional office to Bahrain to be a part of the tender submission. To celebrate this achievement, they organized a memorable dinner event where I was deeply appreciated and acknowledged for my contributions. It was an unforgettable moment and a highlight in my career, marking a significant step forward in our partnership with this Japanese customer.

Obtaining only 15% of their Middle East's total business was a momentous achievement, both personally and for our offices. This accomplishment represented the culmination of persistent efforts and marked a significant milestone in our business journey. It was not only a testament to our dedication and expertise but also a long-awaited success that had a profound impact on our organization and our partnership with them. My packages were revised with more attractive incentive structure with added family benefit and club cards.

The second month after officially establishing our office in Bahrain marked a remarkable achievement for us. We successfully managed the entire event management shipment, involving three chartered flights packed with consignments. Our task was to clear and deliver the cargo on a temporary basis and then re-export it after the conclusion of the Gulf Cup Football event.

Interestingly, it was not our own effort that secured this business; it was our France office that had originally secured the contract. Following a transparent internal policy, the profit from this venture was to be shared equally between the involved parties, and this process was automated. This opportunity proved to be a game-changer for us as it allowed us to cover the entire overhead costs for the year ahead, setting us on a path to financial stability and growth.

While the initial profit from the event management shipment wasn't factored into the branch's achievements, it served as a catalyst for our team. Motivated by this success, we redoubled our efforts and were able to secure more new contractual business and reached profitable starting from the 14th month onwards. This demonstrated our commitment to continuous improvement and our determination to achieve even greater success as a branch.

Working with different management systems from various regions, including European, American, Arabic, and Japanese, has given me unique insights into diverse work cultures. However, the experience of working with Japanese companies stands out as distinct and characterized by a strong emphasis on certain aspects.

In Japanese companies, I found that I had a considerable degree of freedom in terms of how I conducted my work. However, this freedom was balanced by an unwavering commitment to perfect reporting and achieving targets. Reporting in Japanese organizations was a meticulous process, and it often involved asking "3 why's" to dig deep into the root causes of an issue. This emphasis on perfection and precision was a hallmark of Japanese work culture.

I appreciated this aspect of Japanese work culture, even though it could be time-consuming. The commitment to getting things 100% right and the aversion to manipulation instilled a sense of trust and reliability in the work we produced. It also reflected their respect for precision and diligence in their approach to business.

Moreover, I observed that Japanese companies often upheld strong values of respect for all individuals and had a deep-seated commitment to work culture. This manifested in their treatment of employees and colleagues, reflecting a sense of fairness and equality, irrespective of one's background. This culture was something I greatly admired and found enriching in my professional journey.

working with Japanese companies provided a unique experience characterized by an emphasis on perfection, meticulous reporting, a commitment to precision, and a deep respect for humanity and work culture.

Absolutely, when considering a new job opportunity, it's crucial to thoroughly understand and evaluate the work culture. While the potential for higher benefits or compensation can be tempting, it's equally important to assess whether the work environment aligns with your values, needs, and expectations.

A positive work culture not only enhances job satisfaction but also significantly boosts productivity and overall well-being. A supportive and healthy work atmosphere promotes collaboration, innovation, and personal growth. It fosters a sense of belonging, motivation, and job commitment.

In contrast, a toxic or unsuitable work culture can lead to stress, burnout, and dissatisfaction, even if the financial rewards are substantial. Therefore, making an informed decision that takes into account the work culture is essential for long-term career success and personal happiness.

Ultimately, finding a workplace with a good work atmosphere that aligns with your values and goals can lead to a more fulfilling and rewarding professional journey. It's a choice that can have a lasting impact on your career and overall quality of life.

Saying goodbye to Kintetsu World Express after five wonderful years was a bittersweet moment in my career. During this time, I experienced significant achievements and received both moral and financial appreciation. One of the most rewarding aspects of my tenure was the opportunity to officially visit new countries with my family in tow.

Two individuals, Thomas and Uwe, emerged as true heroes in my personal and professional journey. Their roles were pivotal in shaping my career trajectory, and I hold them in high regard. Even after parting ways with the organization, I'm fortunate to maintain a strong and positive communication with these two influential leaders.

Reflecting on my journey, I recognize that in every career path, there must be mentors or guides who play an invaluable role in our development and success. Their guidance and support are indispensable, and I am grateful for the impact they've had on my professional growth. As I bid farewell to one chapter, I eagerly anticipate the opportunities and experiences that lie ahead in my continued journey.

I made the difficult decision to resign from Kintetsu World Express primarily because of my parents, particularly my father. He had suffered a severe stroke that profoundly affected his mental and physical well-being. My father had always been a resilient and strong individual, but after this stroke, his willpower seemed to dwindle, and he required our constant support and presence.

His heartfelt wish was for us, his children, to be by his side during this challenging phase of his life, and he expressed a strong desire to be settled with him in India. It was a decision that I didn't hesitate to make because it felt like the right thing to do. Family is paramount, and being there for my father during his most vulnerable moments was an obligation and a privilege.

I am deeply grateful that the top management at Japan and Netherlands understood the gravity of my situation and accommodated my personal request with utmost compassion. They granted me the flexibility to prioritize my family during this critical time. Their promise that I could return to this Japanese government subsidiary whenever I chose to do so was a testament to the strong bond I had formed with the organization.

Ultimately, my decision to leave this great respectful organization was driven by love and a sense of responsibility towards my family, especially my ailing father. Family values are at the core of who we are, and sometimes, they necessitate making challenging choices.

In 2019, during the peak of the Covid-19 outbreak, the Bahraini government announced the last flight to India from Bahrain. Leveraging my social influence and connections in the airline industry, I managed to secure tickets for my family, allowing us to bid farewell to Bahrain, our home for many years.

Upon our return to India, my initial plan was to venture into farming. However, the reality of the Covid-19 pandemic struck, and I found myself in isolation for a significant period of six to nine months. During this time, I had the opportunity for introspection, and it became evident that farming might not be a suitable path for someone like me who had been engaged in official work continuously for 28 years.

Sometimes, I ponder the idea of embracing retirement for leisure, but I find it to be a rather misleading notion. You see, I'm someone who thrives on routine, meticulously planned schedules, and efficient time management.

The thought of succumbing to a laid-back retirement lifestyle doesn't sit well with me.

Age, in my opinion, is merely a number that we've structured according to our engagements and responsibilities. Take, for instance, someone like me who dutifully heads to the office at 7:30 every morning. Altering this well-established routine might hasten the aging process, making one seem older not just in appearance but in their mindset, activities, and time management as well. Thus, my philosophy is to stay active and adhere to a structured schedule.

Remaining relevant and up-to-date is essential, both in terms of technology and knowledge, as well as staying connected with society and excelling in one's profession. This requires a degree of physical fitness and a well-organized approach to time management.

For those willing to embrace this philosophy, I suggest following the 8+8+8(2x4) approach. Allocate 8 hours for sleep, 8 hours for work or study, and the remaining 8 hours can be divided into various aspects of your life. Dedicate 2 hours to your family, another 2 hours for personal time, set aside 2 hours for maintaining your health, and the final 2 hours for contributing to your society.

In doing so, you not only stay physically fit but also maintain a balanced and fulfilling life. After all, age need not dictate the vitality of our lives; it's how we manage our time and engage with the world that truly matters.

Life has a way of presenting unexpected challenges and opportunities, and my experience during the pandemic was a testament to that. It led me to reevaluate my career and future pursuits, ultimately guiding me in a different direction than I had initially envisioned.

7

ACCREDITATIONS

Over the course of my 30-year professional journey, I have actively sought knowledge and skill enhancement through a myriad of avenues. I've completed and attended numerous inter-organizational training programs as well as external certifications. These experiences have been integral to my continuous learning and professional development. The diverse range of programs has equipped me with a comprehensive skill set, allowing me to navigate and excel in the dynamic landscape of my industry. The commitment to ongoing training reflects my dedication to staying abreast of industry advancements, refining my expertise, and ensuring that I contribute effectively to the organizations I've been a part of. As a result, this wealth of experience and knowledge has become a cornerstone in shaping my approach to challenges and fostering continuous growth throughout my career.

During my tenure with the American company, a significant highlight of my professional development occurred in 1996 when I had the privilege of participating in a training program conducted by Saudi Arabian Airlines. The focus of the program was on the Packing and Handling of Dangerous Goods (DG) cargo. This experience proved to be enlightening, providing me with a profound understanding of the intricacies involved in the handling of DG cargo and the critical role that documentation plays in this process. The training underscored the stringent regulations governing DG cargo and emphasized the paramount importance of adhering to these regulations with precision. The insights gained from the course not only enhanced my competence in safely managing and transporting DG cargo but also instilled in me a deep appreciation for the gravity of compliance in this specialized field. This training experience has since been invaluable in shaping my approach to cargo logistics, particularly in scenarios involving potentially hazardous materials.

Building on the foundational knowledge gained from the training program with Saudi Arabian Airlines, my commitment to excellence in the field of cargo logistics led me to pursue further specialization. Recognizing the importance of staying current with industry standards, I undertook the FIATA Dangerous Goods (DG) Preliminaries course. This advanced training provided a more in-depth exploration of DG regulations, safety protocols, and the intricate details of handling hazardous materials in the logistics chain.

The FIATA DG Preliminaries course equipped me with a comprehensive understanding of the international standards set forth by organizations like the International Air Transport Association (IATA) and other regulatory bodies. This knowledge not only heightened my competence in managing DG cargo but also positioned me as a professional with a nuanced understanding of the legal and operational aspects crucial in the field.

Undertaking this course reflects my dedication to continuous learning and professional development, ensuring that I remain at the forefront of industry best practices. The combined insights from both the Saudi Arabian Airlines training and the FIATA DG Preliminaries course have significantly contributed to my expertise in handling dangerous goods, reinforcing the importance of diligence, compliance, and safety in the intricate world of international logistics.

Regrettably, I couldn't continue my refreshment courses post-2017 due to numerous other pressing engagements. Juggling various commitments has been quite challenging, and unfortunately, it meant putting a pause the FIATA refreshment classes which lead to the expiry of my certification. Despite this, I've garnered a wealth of experience until 2021, and I believe my practical, hands-on involvement has enriched my professional expertise.

In the year 2000, my professional journey took a transformative turn when I immersed myself in a 7-day training program conducted by Archie Global, a prominent South African professional training institute. The program's focal point was the development of Professional Selling Skills, and its impact on my approach to sales was profound.

What set this training experience apart was its meticulous and scientific method of teaching the art of selling. The curriculum unfolded in a systematic manner, guiding participants through each stage of the sales process with precision and clarity. From the initial phase of probing and understanding customer needs to the intricate steps leading up to a successful close, every aspect was meticulously covered. This structured approach provided a roadmap for navigating the complexities of the sales landscape.

What truly made this training exceptional was its commitment to practical application. The program didn't confine itself to theoretical discussions alone. Instead, it incorporated numerous workshops and hands-on activities. Mock sales scenarios allowed participants, including myself, to apply the acquired knowledge in a simulated, yet realistic, environment. These exercises were instrumental in bridging the gap between theory and practical implementation, fostering a deeper understanding of the nuances of professional selling.

The immersive nature of the training left me not only with theoretical insights but also with a toolkit of practical skills that I could immediately apply in real-world sales situations. The workshops provided opportunities to fine-tune my approach, learn from challenges, and refine my techniques under the guidance of experienced trainers.

As I reflect on my professional growth, the Archie Global training program stands out as a cornerstone. It not only equipped me with a systematic and scientific approach to selling but also instilled in me a confidence and proficiency that have been invaluable throughout my career. The blend of theory and practical application in that training program laid the groundwork for my success in the dynamic and ever-evolving field of professional sales.

The Archie Global training program went beyond conventional sales teachings by incorporating dynamic elements that transcended the theoretical realm. One particularly impactful aspect was the hands-on practice of tailoring selling strategies to diverse situations and customer mindsets. This approach was a game-changer, surpassing the depth of understanding I gained during my MBA course.

Engaging in exercises that required us to adapt our selling strategies based on specific scenarios and customer profiles was enlightening. The program emphasized the importance of a spot strategy—something I had not delved into previously. This strategic agility involved discerning the nuances of each interaction, understanding the unique needs and perspectives of different customers, and then crafting a tailored approach on the spot.

What stood out was the practical application of knowledge, honing the ability to swiftly analyze a situation and adjust the sales strategy accordingly. It was more than a theoretical discourse on adapting to diverse customer mindsets; it was a hands-on exploration of the art of situational responsiveness in sales.

Comparatively, my MBA education provided a solid theoretical foundation, but the Archie Global program elevated my understanding to a practical and nuanced level. It brought to light the significance of being agile in the sales process, recognizing that a one-size-fits-all approach is seldom effective. The emphasis on spot strategies underscored the need for adaptability and responsiveness, key elements that significantly impact success in the ever-changing landscape of professional selling.

In retrospect, this aspect of the training program not only broadened my perspective but also became a cornerstone in my approach to sales, shaping my ability to navigate the complexities of diverse customer interactions with confidence and efficacy. The experiential learning at Archie Global was, without a doubt, a transformative supplement to my formal education, offering insights and skills that extended far beyond the conventional teachings of my MBA course.

In my role where I conduct job interviews for MBA graduates, I've observed a notable shift in the quality of education over time. It seems that the current generation of graduates is, to a large extent, more focused on acquiring the MBA title rather than delving into the substance of the education. The process of earning an MBA, which was once a rigorous and demanding journey, now appears to be more accessible, with many graduates seemingly obtaining their degrees without the depth of knowledge and commitment that was characteristic of previous generations.

Back in the day, earning an MBA was a badge of honor that represented not only academic achievement but also a significant investment of time, effort, and intellectual rigor. However, in recent times, the landscape has changed. It's become almost commonplace for individuals to pursue an MBA without a clear vision or genuine commitment to mastering the subject matter.

As someone who has witnessed this trend firsthand, I feel compelled to offer advice to those currently pursuing or contemplating a certification. My suggestion is to go beyond the surface level of education. Instead of merely aiming to pass exams and collect certificates, take the time to truly understand your chosen subject. Consider how the knowledge gained in your course program will be applicable in your career. It's about more than just having a certificate or a title; it's about acquiring a deep understanding of your field and developing practical skills that will set you apart in the professional world.

In today's competitive job market, having an MBA should signify not just a formal qualification but a testament to your expertise and your ability to apply that expertise in real-world scenarios. My recommendation is to approach your certification journey with a mindset focused on depth of understanding and practical application. By doing so, you ensure that your education is not merely a formality but a meaningful investment in your future success and contribution to your chosen industry.

Attending that training program back in 2009 in Australia with the Project Professional group was a game-changer for me. The focus on handling heavy lifts and mega lifts in a cost-effective and professional way really gave me a solid foundation in that niche. The emphasis on remote surveys, understanding potential threats, and being savvy about carrier limitations and equipment specifications made it a well-rounded experience.

Getting that certificate at the end wasn't just a piece of paper—it was like getting a badge of honor. It validated the skills I gained in project cargo handling and mega lifts, which was pretty rewarding.

What's even better is how the training boosted my confidence. It wasn't just about theoretical knowledge; it gave me practical insights that I could directly apply to my work, especially in the realm of project forwarding. It fueled a more assertive approach to sales, which clearly made a positive impact.

I think the specialization that came with that training helped me stand out as an expert in the field. It wasn't just about doing my job; it was about contributing more effectively to projects involving heavy lifts and intricate logistics. That kind of expertise can open doors and lead to exciting opportunities.

Reflecting on that training, I can see how those skills have been a driving force in my career. The industry is always evolving, so staying on top of new developments and advancements has become crucial. Ongoing professional development and keeping an eye on industry trends have become my compass, ensuring that I stay sharp and continue to excel in project forwarding.

Project forwarding knowledge is a cornerstone in the logistics and transportation sector, offering a strategic advantage when orchestrating large-scale projects. This expertise is indispensable due to the inherent complexities involved in managing oversized, heavy, and intricate cargo movements. Professionals well-versed in project forwarding navigate through challenges ranging from regulatory compliance and risk mitigation to optimized cost management. Their proficiency extends to the handling of specialized equipment, ensuring the safe and efficient transport of project cargo. Additionally, project forwarding knowledge encompasses an understanding of global logistics networks, international regulations, and time-sensitive delivery requirements. Effective communication and coordination skills are pivotal, given the need to liaise with diverse stakeholders in the supply chain. Beyond operational considerations, this specialized knowledge contributes to client satisfaction, as successful project execution enhances the reputation of logistics providers. Moreover, the ability to specialize in project forwarding sets professionals apart in the market, positioning them as sought-after experts capable of managing unique and demanding projects. As global trade complexities evolve, the importance of project forwarding knowledge continues to be a linchpin for success in the logistics industry.

In August 2023, I found myself immersed in a transformative 3-day online certification course facilitated by one of the largest network partners in our geographical domain. The course, aptly titled "Remote Selling Skills," was a timely opportunity, especially given the significant shifts in the global sales landscape catalyzed by the Covid-19 pandemic. The program unfolded against the backdrop of a world grappling with unprecedented challenges, and it aimed to equip professionals with the essential skills needed to navigate the evolving dynamics of remote sales.

As the pandemic unfolded, the traditional modes of selling underwent a radical transformation. This course delved into the intricacies of the post-Covid global selling scenario, where sales professionals found themselves categorized into three distinct roles: Online Selling, Hybrid Selling, and Offline Selling. What was once a singular designation on a business card now carried additional nuances that reflected the changing nature of sales engagements.

The "Remote Selling Skills" course was not just a theoretical exploration; it was a practical guide on how to excel in a world where physical interactions were limited. The curriculum covered a spectrum of topics ranging from leveraging advanced virtual communication tools to understanding the psychology of online buyers. The program was designed to enhance our adaptability to a remote working environment, providing insights into effective communication strategies and the art of building relationships virtually.

What made this certification particularly impactful was its real-time relevance. The insights gained weren't just theoretical; they immediately translated into actionable strategies for adapting to the new normal in the sales arena. This training was a testament to the adaptability and resilience required in the face of unprecedented challenges.

Moreover, the recognition of distinct roles—Online, Hybrid, and Offline selling—highlighted the diversification of sales strategies to meet the varied needs of clients and the dynamic nature of the marketplace. The evolution of these categories into designations on business cards underscored the permanence of these changes and the need for sales professionals to be adept at navigating this new terrain.

Undoubtedly, this certification course left an indelible mark on my understanding of modern sales dynamics, providing me with the tools and insights necessary to thrive in an era where remote interactions have become integral to the sales process.

The significance of the "Remote Selling Skills" training became especially pronounced in my role as the leader of a remote team of 25 individuals. In a virtual setting where face-to-face interactions were limited, the insights gained from this training proved instrumental in enhancing my leadership capabilities and empowering my team.

One notable aspect was the practicality of the techniques learned during the course. The step-by-step selling techniques tailored for remote interactions offered a structured approach to engage with clients without the advantage of physical presence. This was particularly valuable for my team, as it equipped them with a systematic methodology to navigate the challenges of remote selling.

The training provided not only theoretical insights but also actionable strategies that could be implemented immediately. As a leader, I found myself armed with effective communication techniques, advanced virtual tools, and a nuanced understanding of online buyer behavior. These tools not only streamlined our sales processes but also boosted the confidence of my team members in the virtual sales arena.

Furthermore, the accessibility of this training was crucial. Recognizing the impracticality of sending all 25 team members for individual courses, especially considering financial constraints in Indian currency, the knowledge gained allowed me to disseminate key learnings and techniques effectively within the team. This approach ensured that the entire team benefitted from the training without incurring prohibitive costs.

In essence, the "Remote Selling Skills" course became a cornerstone in optimizing the performance of my remote team. The techniques acquired not only bolstered our sales strategies but also contributed to the team's cohesion and confidence in navigating the challenges posed by the remote working landscape. The training wasn't just an investment in skill development; it became a catalyst for success in a dynamic and ever-evolving sales environment.

I've had the privilege of participating in more than 24 quality training programs in connection with my seasonal job-related requirements. These programs have covered a wide range of topics, including safety training and ISO auditor training.

These experiences have been instrumental in equipping me with the necessary knowledge and skills to excel in my role and ensure that I meet the required safety and quality standards. I'm committed to continuous professional development and am always eager to expand my expertise to better serve in my seasonal job.

8

DYNAMICS

In the journey of my professional life, I've encountered a diverse array of individuals, each leaving an indelible mark that has shaped my experiences and perspectives. In this book, my intention is to candidly share these encounters, acknowledging the profound impact they've had on both my personal and professional life, either positively or negatively. As someone deeply ingrained in the logistics industry, I am particularly keen on imparting these insights to aspiring professionals entering the dynamic world of logistics.

One of the pivotal themes I aim to explore is the significance of corporate mannerism. I firmly believe that one's conduct within the corporate realm is a critical element in personal and professional development. The book will delve into the nuances of corporate etiquette, illustrating how adherence to certain principles fosters individual growth as an employee. Additionally, I will underscore the ripple effect of such behavior, emphasizing how it extends beyond the individual to directly or indirectly influence the trajectory of the entire organization.

Moreover, I intend to offer practical advice and real-world anecdotes to elucidate the impact of corporate mannerism on organizational outcomes—whether contributing to growth or, conversely, precipitating challenges. Through this narrative, my aim is to provide valuable lessons for young logistics enthusiasts, offering them guidance on navigating the intricate interplay of professional relationships within the corporate landscape.

Ultimately, the book seeks to serve as a mentor, providing insights gleaned from the tapestry of my professional encounters. It is my hope that by sharing these stories, I can contribute to the development of a new generation of professionals who approach their careers with not only competence but also a deep understanding of the human dynamics at play within the corporate sphere.

The first group that falls under the category of the Toxic Underminer poses a significant threat to organizational growth. These individuals, often elevated to managerial positions through inheritance, longstanding tenure, or influential connections, may lack substantive product knowledge. What makes them particularly hazardous is their possessive nature and a reluctance to align with company policies. Operating with a penchant for micro-management, they seek complete control, often manipulating circumstances in their favor through personal connections or ingratiating themselves with higher-ups. These managerial figures frequently disrupt organizational equilibrium for personal gain, driven by a desire to satisfy their ego. The duality of their demeanor is striking: a front face that exudes cordiality, friendliness, and a broad smile, while behind the scenes, they function as corporate snakes, subtly misguiding management and leveraging emotions to serve their own interests. It becomes imperative for organizations to recognize and address such toxicity to maintain a healthy and productive work environment.

Indeed, individuals falling into the Toxic Underminer category often exhibit a stark contrast in their public and private personas. While presenting a friendly and cordial front, their responses to issues are far from gentle; instead, they operate aggressively behind the scenes to manipulate situations in their favor. This aggressive approach not only disrupts the smooth functioning of internal processes within the organization but also creates an atmosphere of toxicity. The paradox lies in their apparent confidence, projecting themselves as knowledgeable, even though their actions may betray a lack of genuine product knowledge. This incongruence often leads to situations where they may face challenges or even insult due to their actual limitations, despite their persistent efforts to portray themselves as all-knowing. Unraveling these dynamics becomes crucial for fostering a healthy workplace culture and preventing the erosion of organizational values.

Individuals falling into the Toxic Underminer category often resort to counterproductive strategies that focus on short-term gains at the expense of long-term growth. One notable tactic is their inclination towards showcasing their managerial prowess through staff reductions or cost-cutting measures instead of actively contributing to revenue generation. This approach, while seemingly demonstrating efficiency to higher-ups, can have detrimental effects on the overall health and sustainability of the organization.

Rather than fostering a culture of innovation and business development, these individuals may prioritize a reductionist mindset that primarily targets operational costs. This approach might lead to a depletion of essential resources, negatively impacting morale, team dynamics, and, ultimately, the organization's ability to thrive. In the long run, such strategies may hinder the company's competitiveness and innovation capacity, undermining its potential for sustainable success.

Identifying and addressing these counterproductive tendencies is crucial for organizations to redirect their focus towards strategies that promote growth, collaboration, and revenue generation, fostering a healthier and more prosperous work environment.

During one of my branch visits in the past company, a junior colleague approached me with some concerning issues related to his manager, whom I've identified as part of the Toxic Underminer category. The problem revolved around a sea shipment that came under a sea waybill with an express release. Despite the express release being in place, the manager insisted on sending a message to the agent to obtain release confirmation. The junior colleague tried explaining the situation, but instead of understanding, the manager became upset and demanded strict compliance with his instructions.

This incident left the junior member in a difficult position, torn between avoiding potential embarrassment in front of counterparts and obeying the manager's directive. It was disheartening to witness the manager's lack of consideration for the valid concerns raised and the unnecessary pressure placed on the junior colleague. This dynamic reflects the toxic nature of such managerial behavior, where personal interests and a need for control override ethical and professional standards.

This situation highlights the challenges posed by individuals in the Toxic Underminer category, as their actions not only jeopardize the well-being of team members but also erode the overall health of the organization. It serves as a stark reminder of the importance of addressing such issues to maintain a workplace culture built on transparency, trust, and ethical conduct.

I've encountered a distinct category of managers whom I'd describe as "Egoistic." Interestingly, these individuals don't necessarily harm the organization outright, but their journey up the career ladder triggers a notable shift in attitude. Starting from the root level, they've grown slowly, and with each step upward, a hidden ego begins to surface, disrupting the once-smooth work climate.

What's intriguing is that their transformation is rooted in their past experiences of being treated poorly and arrogantly. Unfortunately, as they climb the ranks, they tend to perpetuate this behavior, imposing it on their subordinates. One concerning aspect is their inclination to demand reports from a considerable number, if not all, team members—a clear reflection of a hierarchical management style.

On a personal level, these managers are often simple and possess practical experience, particularly in their specific area of expertise. However, their reluctance to delve into other areas of interest can create a challenge in maintaining a collaborative work environment, especially within the confines of an existing hierarchical structure. This dynamic presents a nuanced aspect of organizational behavior that warrants attention and consideration.

To rectify the challenges posed by egoistic managerial behavior, top-level management must adopt strategic resolutions aimed at fostering a healthier workplace culture. Leadership development programs should be implemented, emphasizing emotional intelligence and effective communication to help managers manage their egos and promote collaborative leadership. Cultivating a positive organizational culture, where collaboration, respect, and open communication are valued, is crucial in discouraging arrogant behaviors. Establishing a 360-degree feedback mechanism allows for anonymous employee feedback, offering comprehensive insights into managerial behaviors. Conflict resolution training equips managers with skills to address conflicts constructively, contributing to a more positive work environment. Encouraging cross-functional collaboration and providing opportunities for managers to work on projects outside their expertise broadens perspectives. Clear communication of expectations regarding leadership behavior reinforces the importance of collaborative team-building over hierarchical control. Mentorship programs and regular leadership training refreshers further support ongoing development. Promoting a feedback culture and holding leaders accountable for their behavior ensures a continuous focus on improvement and collaborative leadership. These resolutions collectively contribute to transforming organizational culture, mitigating the negative impact of egoistic managerial behaviors, and fostering a collaborative and positive work environment.

In the intricate tapestry of the professional landscape, there exist individuals whose reservoir of knowledge remains hidden beneath a veneer of humility and selflessness. These colleagues, possessing vast expertise in their respective domains, choose not to flaunt their intellectual prowess within the workplace. Instead, they adopt a generous approach, willingly supporting and imparting knowledge to their peers without contemplating the potential repercussions of their actions.

These unassuming contributors embody a unique blend of altruism and dedication to the collective success of their team. Their selfless acts of teaching and supporting others speak volumes about their commitment to the growth and development of their colleagues. However, this seemingly virtuous approach can, unfortunately, become a double-edged sword.

As these unsung heroes generously share their wealth of knowledge, they may inadvertently neglect to consider the intricate dynamics of workplace politics. Their unassuming nature may render them vulnerable to subtle power plays and manipulations within the organizational structure. In an ironic turn of events, the very people they selflessly supported might turn against them, seizing opportunities to occupy the positions they once held.

The lack of self-promotion and assertiveness might lead to an underestimation of their true value within the organization. Colleagues and superiors, unaware of the depth of their expertise, may fail to recognize their contributions, inadvertently paving the way for others to step into roles that should rightfully be theirs.

To mitigate such risks, these individuals must strike a delicate balance between humility and self-advocacy. While continuing to generously share knowledge, they should also consider actively showcasing their own capabilities and accomplishments. Building a visible and documented track record of their achievements can serve as a safeguard against being overshadowed or undervalued.

Moreover, cultivating an understanding of the organizational dynamics and learning to navigate the intricacies of office politics becomes crucial. Establishing professional boundaries, diplomatically managing relationships, and strategically positioning oneself within the broader context of the workplace are essential skills to prevent their own people from turning against them.

while humility and generosity are admirable traits, professionals with vast knowledge must recognize the importance of asserting themselves within the workplace. It's not merely about occupying a chair or position but ensuring that their contributions are duly acknowledged and that their expertise is recognized as an invaluable asset to the organization.

Managers exhibiting a "yes sir, ok sir" attitude may seemingly survive within an organization without directly harming its sales, profitability, or productivity. However, beneath this façade lies a concealed threat. While these managers may maintain an average level of capacity in key performance areas, their failure to fulfill their prime responsibility—informing or reporting negative or less productive strategies to their superiors—poses a substantial risk.

This lack of transparency can lead to the perpetuation of misguided decisions within the organization. Individuals in this category often refrain from pointing out or escalating truths or valid concerns to the management, driven by a fear of jeopardizing their own positions. Despite their awareness of the potential negative impacts, the prevailing sense of insecurity holds them back from taking a principled stand.

It's crucial to recognize that their loyalty lies more with self-preservation than with a genuine commitment to the organization's well-being. These individuals tend to adopt a passive approach, opting to go with the flow and secure their jobs rather than actively contributing to the organization's success.

To address this issue, management should be astutely aware of and understand this type of behavior. Providing adequate training that emphasizes the importance of open communication, constructive feedback, and the courage to challenge decisions is essential. Alternatively, if this approach proves ineffective, management may need to assess whether retaining such individuals aligns with the organization's values and goals. In cases where their presence hinders the organization's growth or decision-making processes, decisive action, such as reevaluation of roles or removal, may be necessary to ensure the overall health and success of the organization.

Indeed, the presence of managers with a passive "yes sir, ok sir" attitude can have detrimental effects on the overall workplace environment.

Their reluctance to speak up or challenge decisions may create a culture of complacency and inhibit the growth of a vibrant and innovative organizational culture.

One significant consequence is the demotivation of more assertive and sincere colleagues who actively contribute to the organization. Aggressive and committed employees may feel frustrated and undervalued when their efforts go unrecognized or when they witness decisions being made without thorough consideration of all perspectives. This demotivation can have a cascading effect, leading to decreased morale, lower productivity, and potentially driving talented individuals to reconsider their commitment to the organization.

In many cases, when dedicated employees perceive a lack of values or a stifling atmosphere within the organization, they may choose to leave. The departure of such individuals not only results in a loss of valuable talent but can also contribute to a negative cycle, where the absence of motivated and skilled team members further erodes the organizational culture.

Addressing this issue requires a multifaceted approach. Management should not only recognize and rectify the behavior of passive managers but also actively promote a culture that values openness, transparency, and constructive feedback. Encouraging and rewarding proactive contributions from employees can help build a positive work environment and prevent the demotivation of sincere and dedicated team members. Regular communication channels, such as feedback sessions and performance reviews, can provide a platform for recognizing and appreciating the efforts of high-performing employees. Ultimately, fostering a culture that values and supports its employees can contribute to a more engaged and motivated workforce. Unfortunately, we can find at least one or two such characters in every organization.

The internal threat emerging from employees engaging in unethical practices, specifically accepting financial incentives from vendors and carriers in exchange for divulging confidential information, presents a profound challenge for the organization. These actions not only compromise the ethical foundation of the organization but also pose significant risks to its financial stability and reputation within the industry. The organization's response, characterized by decisive measures such as termination and legal actions against those implicated, reflects a commitment to maintaining integrity and trust. Unfortunately, we could see one like in every organization.

To effectively address this ongoing threat, it is essential to adopt continuous vigilance and preventive measures. Robust internal controls, including regular audits, can serve as crucial tools to detect and deter unethical behavior. However, beyond these structural mechanisms, fostering a culture of transparency and integrity is paramount. Employees should feel empowered to report any suspicious activities through confidential channels, creating a collaborative effort to safeguard the organization's values.

Communication becomes a linchpin in this effort. Clearly conveying the severe consequences of betraying the organization's trust underscores the commitment to upholding a fair and ethical workplace. Training initiatives on ethical conduct and data security not only equip employees with the knowledge to navigate ethical dilemmas but also contribute to building a collective ethos of responsibility.

The organization's swift and decisive actions in response to breaches of trust send a resounding message about the non-negotiable nature of ethical standards. This reinforces the importance of trust and accountability within the workplace, establishing a precedent that unethical behavior will not be tolerated. In essence, confronting this internal threat requires a multifaceted approach that combines structural safeguards, cultural reinforcement, and swift corrective actions to preserve the organization's integrity and long-term success.

The pivotal role played by experienced managers possessing profound knowledge in geography, product, and effective man-management cannot be overstated. These individuals stand as the linchpin of any organization, serving not merely as managers but as inspirational leaders who lead their teams from the forefront. Their expertise extends beyond the superficial, encompassing a deep understanding of geographical nuances, the intricacies of the products or services offered, and the art of effective people management.

These managers, as true assets to the organization, assume leadership responsibilities with a sense of accountability. They lead by example, stepping forward to shoulder responsibilities in times of error and graciously attributing success to the collective efforts of their team members. In their mentorship role, they impart valuable knowledge to their teams, fostering a culture of continuous learning and growth.

What sets these individuals apart is their ability to formulate and execute effective strategies that contribute to the overall development of the team. They operate with a shared vision, aligning their efforts with organizational policies and regulations. Their leadership style not only motivates team members but also creates an environment where each individual is recognized and credited for their contributions.

This book introduces readers to some of these remarkable individuals, serving as genuine motivators and guides in the professional realm. My personal experiences, woven into the narrative, highlight the positive impact these leaders have had on the organization and, undoubtedly, on the professional journey of mine. The enjoyment derived from these interactions underscores the profound influence that effective leadership can have on individual experiences within the organization.

The rapid pace of my personal growth undoubtedly finds its roots in the profound influence of the exceptional personalities I encountered throughout my professional journey. These leaders and mentors, who epitomized strong values and effective leadership, played a pivotal role in shaping my outlook. By embracing their values and internalizing the lessons drawn from their experiences, I navigated my own path of development.

Leaders who lead with accountability, acknowledge errors, and credit their teams for accomplishments create a culture of collaboration and continuous improvement. If my journey reflects these principles, it's a testament to the impact of positive role models. Their influence extends beyond the professional realm, shaping my personal ethos and contributing to my overall growth.

Taking a moment to reflect on the values and strategies instilled by these influential personalities allows me to appreciate the profound effect they've had on my trajectory. As I continue to evolve both professionally and personally, the lessons learned from these mentors remain a guiding force in my ongoing journey of growth and success.

9

BACK HOME

After spending an extended period at home during the COVID-19 isolations and lockdowns, I began to feel a sense of restlessness and a desire to re-engage with life. I discussed this with one of my friends, and together, we decided to embark on a new venture. my initial idea was to set up a small office in Kochi, the financial capital of Kerala, and started conducting market research to explore our options. Given my limited knowledge of import customers due to my long service in the Middle East region, I decided to focus on the export business.

As we delved deeper into the planning and execution of our startup, I had the opportunity to connect with many my old clients in Middle-East involved in exporting goods from India. The journey was both exciting and challenging as we navigated the intricacies of the export market.

During this period of progress and growth, I had the pleasure of meeting Mr. Sunil Kumar, who works in a Middle East based logistics organization as its group HR, a well-established family business in the Middle East. Our discussions about the various business activities were going well, and he extended a kind invitation to visit their facilities and learn more about their operations. I wholeheartedly accepted his invitation and promised to make the visit during my upcoming trip to Ernakulam.

This encounter with him and the prospect of visiting their office added an exciting dimension to my future vision. It's a testament to the power of networking and the unexpected opportunities that can arise when you're open to new experiences and collaborations.

As I mentioned before, individuals like Mr. Jean, Uwe, and Thomas have had a profound influence on me throughout my life. Sunil, on the other hand, quickly emerged as another personality who resonated with me on a deep level. Within a short period of knowing each other, it became evident that we shared a similar wavelength, and at times, it felt as though there was a telepathic connection between us.

As the days went by, Sunil and his family became an integral part of our lives. We not only discussed business matters but also delved into personal issues, offering support and finding resolutions together. Our relationship extended beyond professional connections, and we became like an extended family to one another. It's moments like these, where genuine connections are formed, that truly enrich one's life and make the journey all the more rewarding.

After 20 days, I had the opportunity to visit his office, located in Malappuram district, approximately 13 kilo meters away from the famous Guruvayur temple. The moment I laid eyes on the office, was struck by its beauty. It was a five-story building situated amidst a sprawling plot adorned with coconut trees, with an endless paddy field stretching out beside it. The setting was nothing short of breathtaking, a workplace where the natural surroundings could effortlessly alleviate any work-related stress. Nature's influence on decision-making is undeniable, from environmental impact considerations to well-being, agriculture, disaster preparedness, conservation, culture, and ethics. It's an integral part of our choices, reflecting our deep interdependence with the natural world.

A few minutes later, Sunil came down to greet me, and we engaged in discussions on various topics, mostly unrelated to the industry, delving into personal matters as we discovered we hailed from the same district in Kerala. During our lengthy conversation, he surprised me by suggesting or forcing that I take on the role of the commercial head within the organization. He believed my experience could bring significant value to the team. This unexpected proposition left me in a state of confusion, especially because I had been planning to launch my own business. Sunil had placed me in a challenging dilemma. After much thought, deliberations and contemplation, I informed him that I needed some time to consider his proposal before giving him an answer.

he provided a clear explanation of his MD's vision and social commitment, particularly in establishing a facility in a village area. This demonstrates a strong dedication to a cause, highlighting a commitment that seems to be dwindling in today's society. Emotions and values related to social responsibility and community support sometimes appear to be fading away in our increasingly fast-paced and individualistic world. It's encouraging to see individuals like Sunil and his MD who continue to prioritize such important values and actions in their endeavors. also emphasized Nassar's deep sense of support for old parents, which is another dimension of his commitment to social values. In today's society, the tradition of caring for elderly family members often faces challenges as priorities shift. In fact that matches with my own views.

Later, I found myself in the fortunate position of meeting the Managing Director of the organization, Mr. BP Nassar, a dynamic and young personality radiating an abundance of positive energy. Our conversation gone into the big world of the logistics industry, covering a wide range of topics, including commonly known figures for both of us.

In the logistics industry, a unique camaraderie exists among professionals, even when they compete fiercely in the marketplace. This is because, over time, individuals within the industry tend to build networks and connections that transcend competitive boundaries. It's a tight-knit community where industry insiders often share insights, experiences, and even friendships despite their companies being in direct competition with each other

During the long conversation, Sunil has emphasized the job offer he tabled on and my vision. I had only one condition for accepting the offer - I needed the freedom to make my mark within the organization, to leave my own unique imprint. It was important to me that I could contribute in a meaningful way and make a difference.

In my opinion, when considering a transition to a new organization, especially for a senior position, it's essential to assess whether you'll have the opportunity to make meaningful contributions to that organization and face new challenges. Merely joining a company to follow established procedures or adhere to policies that you believe are flawed can be a frustrating endeavour. It's crucial to aim for a role where you can thrive and showcase your capabilities, benefiting both yourself and the organization.

The key is to identify areas where you can bring value and innovation to the organization. Seek opportunities to address gaps or shortcomings, whether it's in processes, strategies, or leadership. However, it's equally important to evaluate whether the challenges you'd face are manageable. If the task seems insurmountable or if the organization's culture and hierarchy hinder your ability to enact positive change, it may be wise to reconsider your decision.

Many organizations have entrenched hierarchies and individuals who resist change because they're comfortable with the status quo. Middle management, often responsible for implementing changes, may remain silent due to the fear of disrupting the organization's stability for short time. In such cases, it's essential to weigh your potential impact against the likelihood of success. If the odds are against you, it might be more productive to explore other opportunities where your skills and ideas can flourish. After all, your career should be a path of growth and fulfilment, not one of constant frustration and stagnation.

During a challenging period when my brother-in-law was battling cancer, I found myself at the hospital, serving as a bystander and offering support. It was during this difficult time that Sunil informed me about a call from Mr. Vivian Castellano, the Regional Director of the organization. Despite my circumstances, I took the call and interacted with him and also explaining my situation.

Mr. Vivian is a remarkable individual, now 65 years old. I discovered many admirable qualities in him - he's genuinely compassionate, a great mentor, and an excellent teacher. Despite my 29 years of professional experience, there were still many lessons I had yet to learn, and he became a source of valuable insights. His approach to organizing and conducting meetings, his introductions of team members, and his unwavering commitment to tasks and follow-ups were all noteworthy.

Initially, he approaches to my work may have seemed demanding and even somewhat annoying. However, when I expressed my feelings, he explained that his intention was to toughen me up and instil a greater sense of organization in my work. This perspective completely changed my perception of him, and my respect for him grew exponentially. He pushed me to take on new challenges and consistently acknowledged my efforts. At times, he even encouraged me to refine my communication style, emphasizing the importance of such refinement for my position within the organization.

In Vivian, I found not only a mentor but also a guide who helped me evolve both professionally and personally. His influence on my career and development was profound, and I am deeply grateful for the lessons he imparted and the growth he facilitated.

Mr. Vivian Castellino's boundless energy and enthusiasm, as mentioned earlier, perfectly exemplify the notion that "age is just a number." One remarkable aspect of his life that truly inspired me and served as a catalyst for writing this book was his pursuit of a Ph.D. in Supply Chain Management at the age of 63.

His decision to undertake such a significant academic endeavour at an age when many might consider slowing down was nothing short of awe-inspiring. It made me reflect on my own potential and aspirations. If Vivian could embark on this journey of continuous learning and growth at 64, why couldn't I? It dawned on me that age should never be a barrier to pursuing one's dreams and ambitions.

This realization became the cornerstone of my motivation for writing this book, particularly for those in the logistics profession. Dr. Vivian Castellino's story serves as a testament to the fact that there is always room for growth, learning, and achievement, regardless of one's age. His example encourages others in the field to adopt a similar mindset of continuous improvement and to embrace new challenges with enthusiasm.

Ultimately, this book aims to inspire and motivate logistics professionals to recognize their own potential and to embrace lifelong learning and development, just as Dr. Vivian did. Age should never be a deterrent; instead, it should be a source of motivation to keep pushing boundaries and striving for excellence in the logistics industry.

It's fascinating how life can sometimes bring people together in unexpected ways. The coincidence of me and Dr. Vivian attending the same conference in 1997 in Dubai while working for same organizations but in different countries is a remarkable example of such occurrences. It's a testament to how small the world can feel at times and how seemingly unrelated paths can cross in surprising ways.

These kinds of coincidences can be quite striking and often serve as a reminder of the interconnectedness of our experiences and the people we encounter throughout our lives. They can also make for interesting stories and add a layer of intrigue to our personal and professional relationships.

It's always a delightful experience to uncover these shared moments from the past and recognize the various ways in which our paths may have crossed, even if we were unaware of it at the time. It's a reminder of the many stories and connections that make up the tapestry of our lives.

Despite the fact that the position offered was much lower than my previous role, I didn't hesitate to accept. There was something about the environment and the people that drew me in and the deep feeling that I could do some significant changes here.

Upon assuming my new role as Senior Commercial Manager, I continued with a strategy that had served me well throughout my career – building a network of trustworthy individuals across all departments and branches. This strategy may be considered unconventional by some, but for my position, it was crucial in obtaining valuable information. I had learned this approach from Mr. Jean and had successfully implemented it in previous organizations. It allowed me to tap into the knowledge of root-level employees who often possessed insights that never made their way to the top echelons of management.

Here at the Back office, I began to gather even the most minute pieces of information, both positive and negative, as it provided me with a comprehensive view of the organization's inner workings. I engaged with numerous individuals across various branches, seeking to understand their perspectives and requirements.

After conducting a thorough SWOT analysis, I uncovered a multitude of opportunities that presented themselves as key avenues for my active involvement, particularly in steering the company towards substantial growth and corporate prominence. The analysis illuminated areas where my skills, expertise, and strategic insights could be leveraged to capitalize on emerging prospects. This revelation not only highlighted the potential for my impactful contributions but also positioned me as a vital player in shaping the trajectory of the company as it aspired to transform into a corporate powerhouse. The SWOT analysis served as a strategic compass, guiding me toward avenues where my interventions could be most influential in fostering the company's advancement and long-term success.

Mr. Nassar is a remarkable leader, known for his friendly demeanour and visionary thinking. His ability to dream big and then take concrete steps to turn those dreams into reality is a rare quality, especially in the business world. I've witnessed firsthand his passion and determination to elevate the company to greater heights.

Throughout my tenure, I've had occasions to discuss the company's potential and the areas where improvements could be made. I've often pointed out, either directly or indirectly, instances where revenues were not being optimized to their fullest potential. However, I refrain from delving into the specifics in this book, as it's not my intention to create a controversy.

My focus here is on sharing the positive aspects of our journey and the lessons learned along the way. While every organization faces its challenges, it's equally important to highlight the strengths and successes that contribute to its growth and prosperity. Through this book, I hope to inspire and motivate others in the logistics profession while maintaining a respectful and constructive tone.

Over time, I gradually became more closely involved in numerous activities within the organization. This increased participation led to the development of a trust factor between myself and the administration. As I became more engaged in various aspects of the organization's operations, a sense of trust and reliability was cultivated, fostering a stronger connection between me and the management. The privilege of being chosen to represent the company at numerous conferences and serve as the organization's ambassador was an extraordinary honor that left a profound impact on me. It went beyond a mere acknowledgment of my efforts; it was a tangible expression of the value placed on the work I had tirelessly invested in the company. The fact that both the CEO and COO had entrusted me with such a responsibility was not only a recognition of my dedication but also a clear indication that my contributions were not just noticed but deeply appreciated. This opportunity to represent the organization at high-profile events underscored the trust and confidence they had in my abilities, further motivating me to continue striving for excellence in my role. Such opportunities to represent a company at conferences and events are not only a testament to one's dedication and expertise but also a chance to showcase the organization's strengths and capabilities on a broader stage. It's a mark of trust and confidence in an individual's ability to effectively represent the company and communicate its vision and values to a wider audience.

In my life, I never considered myself much of a traveller. However, I've had the opportunity to explore nearly 34 different countries, strictly on business, sometimes with family as well. For me, alongside my other hobbies like collecting caps, airline miniatures, and coins, I developed a new fascination of collecting airline boarding passes. It all started with a conversation I had with Mr. Kamal during one of our rare personal talks.

During many occasions, Dr. Vivian expressed his own ambitious goal to visit 100 countries in his lifetime. As someone who has been inspired by him personally and follows in his footsteps, I can't help but think that perhaps I too could aspire to such a remarkable milestone, if God allows. Dr. Vivian, at this age, continues to nurture his adventurous spirit, and it's a testament to the fact that age should never be a barrier to pursuing one's dreams and exploring the wonders of the world.

One year after joining, I found myself a member of the executive board, shouldering a multitude of responsibilities. In this role, I had to approach matters from a neutral standpoint, offering opinions and arguments that served the best interests of the organization as a whole. However, despite my impartial stance, some within the group believed that I was advocating for only one side, even though many times my stance was aligned with what was right for the organization.

Navigating such perceptions and maintaining objectivity in a leadership role can be challenging. It's essential to continue making decisions and offering insights that are grounded in the organization's best interests, even in the face of misconceptions. Over time, consistent and principled leadership can help demonstrate your commitment to the organization's success, gradually dispelling any doubts about your intentions.

In my tenure at this organization, I had the privilege of taking on a role that went beyond my daily tasks in logistics. It involved mentoring and guiding students from the esteemed Logistics Academy, a sister concern, a responsibility I embraced wholeheartedly. This opportunity allowed me to impart not just theoretical knowledge but also practical wisdom gained from my own extensive experience in the logistics industry.

Training these students of the practical intricacies of freight forwarding was just the tip of the iceberg. I wanted them to be well-prepared for the challenges they would inevitably encounter in the dynamic world of logistics. Thus, it was essential to instil in them a deep understanding of the industry's ethical standards and practices. Emphasizing the importance of a strong code of ethics was a cornerstone of my mentorship. I wanted them to appreciate the significance of conducting business with integrity, transparency, and respect for all stakeholders.

Moreover, discipline in logistics cannot be overstated. In a field where precision and efficiency are paramount, along with my team, I worked with the students to develop a disciplined approach to their work. This involved time management, attention to detail, and a commitment to delivering results consistently.

One of the most gratifying aspects of this experience has been the enduring connections I forged with these students. Beyond their graduation and entry into the logistics profession, many continued to reach out to me when facing challenges or issues in their work. They viewed me not only as a mentor but as a trusted advisor, and their trust in seeking my guidance was both humbling and rewarding. This lasting impact on their professional journeys has been a source of great satisfaction and underscores the significance of mentorship in fostering meaningful and enduring relationships.

I've encountered numerous occasions where former students reached out to me months after their graduation, especially if they faced challenges securing a job in the industry. In these instances, I consistently offered my support by leveraging my professional network and personal connections within the industry. It has been a great experience to not only mentor to students during their academic journey but to continue assisting them as they transition into the professional world, using my connections to help them navigate the job market and find suitable opportunities. This commitment to ongoing support underscores the importance of building lasting relationships beyond the training sessions.

These connections serve as a testament to the enduring impact we can have on the logistics community. Our knowledge and experiences, shared generously with the next generation, have the power to shape the future of the industry. It's a reminder that our contributions extend beyond our immediate roles and responsibilities, echoing through the careers of those we've mentored.

In recent times, due to my active participance in social media like LI, FB and Insta, I've found myself fielding numerous inquiries from logistics graduates scattered across different parts of India. What's surprising is not the sheer volume of calls but the common thread running through them—anxiety and uncertainty about the quality of education provided by logistics institutions. This realization has sparked concerns about whether these educational endeavours are genuinely designed to impart knowledge and skills or if they are merely *profit-driven* endeavours doling out *paper certificates.*

The logistics and supply chain industry, often referred to as the backbone of a country's GDP, is undeniably vital. Yet, it seems that many aspiring professionals are entering the field without a solid understanding of the industry's demands or the requisite skill set. As someone who has fielded these calls, I feel a responsibility to shed light on how aspiring logistics professionals can equip themselves for success and, crucially, how they can make a meaningful entry into the industry.

Firstly, it's crucial to identify institutions that go beyond a superficial curriculum. Seek out those that offer a comprehensive, 360-degree view of the industry. The curriculum should encompass not only theoretical aspects but also practical knowledge. Look for programs that cover product knowledge, geographical considerations, and the intricacies of port and airport operations.

Internships is nothing to do for mending professionals but a practical training should be integrated into the educational journey. Real-world experience is invaluable in a dynamic industry like logistics. It's not enough to understand concepts in theory; one must be able to apply them in the field. This hands-on experience is where true learning occurs.

Soft skills often take a backseat in discussions about logistics education, but they are equally crucial. Effective communication, teamwork, problem-solving, and leadership are essential components of a successful career in logistics. Graduates must be equipped with these skills to navigate the complex and collaborative nature of the industry.

Choosing an educational institution that offers career counselling and placement assistance is paramount. Graduates need guidance on the diverse career paths within the logistics sector and assistance in securing internships and job placements. This connection between education and industry placement ensures that the transition from academia to the professional world is smooth and seamless.

Now, regarding how to enter the logistics industry or secure a job, networking becomes even more important. Actively participate in Profession social media platforms, seminars/webinars, and workshops. Building a network of contacts within the logistics community opens doors to opportunities, provides insights, and fosters a sense of community. Additionally, consider reaching out to professionals in the field for informational interviews or mentorship.

education in logistics should be seen as an investment in one's career and future. By choosing institutions that offer a comprehensive education, including theoretical knowledge, practical experience, soft skills development, and networking opportunities, aspiring logistics professionals can position themselves for success in an industry that is the lifeblood of the nation's economy. It's time to prioritize the quality of education over the allure of certificates, ensuring that the logistics professionals of tomorrow are truly prepared for the challenges and opportunities that lie ahead and equipped with the strategies to make a meaningful entry into this dynamic industry.

I want to emphasize that my recognition of the academy's effectiveness is not solely because I am employed here; rather, it stems from the fact that our institute stands out as one of the two providing the comprehensive 360-degree education and real time work experience to equip the new generation. The academy's commitment to offering a well-rounded education, covering both theoretical knowledge and practical skills, sets it apart. This holistic approach ensures that students not only grasp the theoretical foundations of logistics but also gain hands-on experience, preparing them thoroughly for the challenges of the real-world logistics landscape.

As I reflect on this chapter of my career, I look forward with enthusiasm to the ongoing journey of mentorship and collaboration. The logistics industry is ever-evolving, and as we continue to share knowledge and support one another, we can collectively navigate the challenges and seize the opportunities that lie ahead.

As part of our efforts to create a more corporate and structured climate within the organization, significant changes were made to the management designations. In this restructuring, I had the honor of being appointed as the Chief Commercial Officer (CCO). This new role came with no increased responsibilities and a broader scope in guiding and shaping the commercial aspects of the company. It marked a significant step in our journey towards becoming a more corporate and efficiently organized entity.

While working with this organization, as opposed to my experience in previous companies, I've had the fortune of interacting with employees at various levels within the their daily activities, especially in marketing and operation departments which comes under my domain along with some other departments, many of whom were at a very junior level with little to no experience, ranging from newcomers to those with just a year of experience. This presented a valuable opportunity for me to share my own experiences and insights to catalyze their growth in respective area.

In this environment, I took it upon myself to mentor and train these individuals, steering them away from the traditional approaches to marketing and operations. Instead of relying on generic email blasts and introductory messages, I encouraged them to carve out their own selling strategies. The focus was on empowering them to think creatively rather than adhering strictly to strategies crafted by others. How many of them benefited from this was out of the question, but most of them informed me at a later stage or after they joined another organization about the increased efficiency due to the training.

Throughout our training sessions, I consistently emphasized the importance of aligning their strategies with both company policies and the specific characteristics of their target customer. I often reminded them that a one-size-fits-all approach doesn't work in sales. Flexibility and adaptability are key when it comes to tailoring strategies to the unique needs and preferences of individual clients.

The recurring metaphor in my mentorship was the powerful analogy that "using old keys won't open new locks." This metaphor encapsulates a fundamental principle, especially relevant in the ever-evolving landscape of logistics. In an industry that thrives on adaptability and innovation, adhering rigidly to outdated or conventional methods can impede progress and hinder success. To instill this idea in the team, I urged them to move away from established norms and embrace a more dynamic approach.

Moreover, I stressed the importance of not just reveling in our victories but, more critically, dedicating time to dissecting the reasons behind losses. Failures, when analyzed thoughtfully, act as invaluable teachers. By delving into the root causes of setbacks, the team could not only mitigate future negatives but also cultivate a culture of continuous improvement. This analytical mindset serves as a catalyst for long-term success, fostering resilience and adaptability in the face of challenges. In encouraging the team to view failures as opportunities for learning and growth, the aim was to cultivate a proactive and forward-thinking mindset within the dynamic field of logistics.

This approach aimed not only at building a more effective sales team but also fostering a culture of innovation and adaptability within the organization. Through this journey, I witnessed firsthand the transformation of these junior logistics professionals into more strategic, independent thinkers capable of navigating the complexities of the industry.

I want to stress the importance of a strong work ethic and dedication, especially to young logisticians. Don't solely focus on seeking appreciation; it will naturally come your way if you consistently give your best to your work.

Drawing from my own experiences, I've faced challenges and even resistance from colleagues, but I never let that deter me. I stayed committed to my responsibilities and worked diligently.

The key lesson here is to be proactive and dedicated without expecting immediate recognition. Over time, your efforts will shine through, and your contributions will be acknowledged. It's a valuable principle for not only young logisticians but anyone looking to excel in their careers.

"**Stop being worried of what could go wrong just start being exited of what could you do**", I've come to adopt this philosophy of *Tommy Robbins*, that centres around facing challenges with a fearless spirit, unburdened by the worries of what might go wrong. This perspective stems from a deep belief that waiting for ideal circumstances or guaranteed success often leads to missed opportunities and unrealized potential.

My story stands as a testament to the transformative power of taking initiative and confronting uncertainties head-on. I've chosen not to let the fear of potential setbacks dictate my actions, and, as a result, I've navigated through a variety of situations, each presenting its unique challenges and learning opportunities. Along the way, I've encountered both successes and setbacks, but through it all, I've learned, adapted, and continued to move forward.

The essence of my journey lies in the understanding that waiting for assurance or perfect conditions can hinder progress and personal growth. Life is dynamic, filled with unpredictability, and my experiences have shown me that meaningful progress often emerges from the willingness to step into the unknown.

By sharing my experiences, I hope to inspire others to embrace a similar mindset — to take that first step, confront challenges, and learn from the journey. My story is an invitation to reject the notion of waiting for the perfect moment, recognizing that the richness of life is often found in the courage to act, the willingness to learn, and the acceptance that growth is an ongoing journey with both highs and lows

I'm feeling really good about my decision to take a sabbatical. It's not something I'm worrying about at all. I believe it's the right choice for me at this point in my life. It's a chance to take a break from my regular routine, recharge, meeting old friend, grow more socially and explore new opportunities. Following the footsteps of Dr. Vivian, I wish to attempt for PHD as well. I see it as a chance for personal growth, gaining fresh perspectives, write some books related to industry and finding a new sense of purpose. I've thought this through and have a clear plan for how I want to spend my sabbatical. I'm looking forward to this time to relax, learn, and do things that truly make me happy. I know sabbaticals are essential for maintaining work-life balance and overall well-being, and I'm excited about the journey ahead!

In this chapter, it is imperative to address the meticulous handling of illegal, ammunition or restricted cargo, emphasizing the absolute necessity for adherence to legal compliance in both the country of export and the destination country. Failure to incorporate such information would render the book incomplete. A poignant example from my own experiences underscores the gravity of this matter. During my tenure here, a colleague, whether intentionally or inadvertently and without managerial consent, dispatched a shipment from Dubai to Saudi Arabia. Although the shipment was documented as network cables, its actual contents were cigarettes—an item restricted for import into Saudi Arabia. To import cigarettes into KSA required approvals and special permission and need to pay huge duties. This incident serves as a stark reminder of the repercussions that can arise when deviating from legal protocols in international trade. Not only did this breach potentially incur fines, shipment rejection and legal actions against the organization, but it also underscored the vital importance of obtaining management approval before the shipment of potentially problematic cargo. Including such practical scenarios in the narrative not only adds a cautionary dimension to the guide but also reinforces the responsibility of individuals in cargo management to ensure legal compliance and maintain the integrity of the logistics process.

it is crucial to instil an acute awareness of international legal protocols. While memorization is not the primary goal, the imperative is to engrain the understanding that, before executing any shipment, thorough preparation is non-negotiable. Adopting a preventative mindset becomes paramount, as the adage *"prevention is better than cure"* holds particular relevance in the realm of logistics. Acknowledging the potential for misinformation or lack of knowledge regarding cargo contents, it becomes imperative to exercise diligent control. Documentation emerges as a key tool not only to safeguard individual interests but also to protect the broader organizational stakes. This proactive approach serves as a vital layer of defence against inadvertent oversights or intentional misrepresentations, reinforcing the principle that a well-informed and meticulous logistician is an asset in navigating the complex landscape of international trade.

As I reach the end of this book, I want to highlight a deliberate choice—to reserve some unfulfilled efforts for the final chapters. These aspirations are not failures but was not able to accomplish due to many reasons and I need to fulfill in the future. They signify my unwavering commitment to continue pursuing excellence in logistics, no matter the challenges. As I move forward in my career, I carry these dreams with me, ready to transform them into accomplishments. The logistics industry is a area of boundless potential, and these aspirations are a evident to that. They serve as a reminder that the journey continues, and I eagerly anticipate what lies ahead.

During the years 2006-2008, a compelling vision took shape—a vision that would embody the essence of collaboration and global connectivity within the logistics industry. This was the time when I embarked on a remarkable thought to establish a Freight forwards Network, the World Logistics Link (WLL). I gone ahead with some of my know people in the freight industry, they are from different parts of the world indeed.

Our shared passion for logistics brought us together, and we were determined to create something extraordinary. WLL wasn't merely a business venture; it was a collective dream that we were determined to turn into reality. With this goal in mind, we set out to pool our resources, knowledge, and expertise to create an independent forwarder network headquartered in the vibrant city of Hong Kong.

The effort was marked by unwavering determination and a strong sense of purpose. We officially registered WLL, but that was just the beginning. Our vision was clear—to expand this network and build a global community of logistics professionals who shared our enthusiasm for this initiative. In June 2008, we hosted our inaugural conference in Hong Kong with 28 members, bringing together individuals who were as passionate about this venture as we were.

Our commitment was solid, and we set an ambitious target—to recruit a minimum of 100 members within one year. Each member, including myself, devoted their time, effort, and resources to make WLL a resounding success.

The enthusiasm and dedication of our initial members were palpable, and we had every reason to believe that our dream was attainable.

However, the global financial recession that swept across the world in 2009-10 posed an unforeseen and monumental challenge. It tested the resilience of industries worldwide, and our initiative was no exception. Despite our best efforts, the recession's impact was profound, affecting not only our founding members but also those who had pledged to join our network.

As the recession's grip tightened, some of our executive members, with the exception of a dedicated few, found it increasingly difficult to fulfil their commitments. Despite the setbacks, we persevered, fuelled by our unshakeable belief in the potential of WLL.

Ultimately, the external economic forces became insurmountable, and we were compelled to make the painful decision to let go of the initiative. While it was a challenging moment, it's vital to recognize that this journey was defined not by its conclusion but by the courage, determination, and vision that brought us together in the first place.

The story of *World Logistics Link* stands as a testament to the spirit of innovation, collaboration, and resilience that defines the logistics industry. It serves as a reminder that even in the face of adversity, the seeds of inspiration and ambition continue to thrive, awaiting the right time to be nurtured once again.

The chapter of WLL may have come to a close, but its legacy endures in the indomitable spirit of the logistics community. Our commitment to excellence, our dedication to forging global connections, and our unwavering belief in the power of collaboration remain unshaken, serving as a beacon of hope and inspiration for future endeavours in the world of logistics

One of the most rewarding aspects of my journey in the logistics industry has been the chance to inspire and guide the next generation, particularly my daughter, Spatha. From her earliest years, she displayed a profound interest in logistics, a passion she has carried with her into adulthood.

As she completes her studies and delves into the complexities of this dynamic field, I will make a deliberate choice to support her in experiencing the industry from its very foundation. I will encourage her to begin at the grassroots level, to learn the ropes, and to confront the challenges head-on. It will be my way of ensuring that she understands every facet of this intricate world. By the time I need to restart WLL, she will have gained valuable experience and insight into the logistics industry, making her a valuable asset to the initiative.

As someone said ***"Life is not measured by the breaths we take, but by the moments that take our breath away."***

10

SABBATICAL

As I look back on the past three decades of my life dedicated to the world of logistics, I am reminded of the countless challenges, triumphs, defeats and lessons learned along the way. My journey in this dynamic field has been a testament to the power of adaptability, innovation, and resilience. From navigating the complexities of global supply chains to finding creative solutions to seemingly insurmountable problems, I've discovered that logistics is not just about moving goods; it's about connecting people, businesses, and opportunities. With each passing year, my passion for this ever-evolving industry has only deepened, and I'm more convinced than ever that logistics is the heartbeat of modern commerce. As I conclude this book of my career, I am filled with gratitude for the incredible individuals and experiences that have shaped me. *The road ahead may be uncertain*, but I'm ready to embrace new challenges and continue pushing the boundaries of what's possible.

As I reflect on my experiences as a logistician, I find myself compelled to share the lessons I've learned, both the highs and the lows, with the next generation. In today's world, where there seems to be a reluctance to embrace life's pressures and a tendency to avoid investing time wholeheartedly, especially in solving the intricate challenges of moving shipments, I feel a calling to pass on my insights.

It's disheartening to see some shy away from the demanding nature of our field. However, I firmly believe in the power of a positive mindset and a steadfast approach to problem-solving. In my journey, I've come to see challenges not as roadblocks but as opportunities to discover solutions. It's akin to finding the right key for every lock — a process that demands patience and dedication.

Frustration, I've learned, is not a remedy. Rather, it's a signal that there's work to be done. Every problem, no matter how daunting, holds a solution waiting to be uncovered. I want to instil in the upcoming generation the belief that with patience and a dedicated approach, they can unravel even the most complex logistical puzzles.

In the future, my aspiration is to be a guide and mentor, offering training that goes beyond the technical aspects of logistics. I want to share not only the successes but also the challenges I faced, creating a realistic picture of our dynamic industry. By doing so, I hope to inspire a new breed of logisticians who not only possess the necessary skills but also approach their work with resilience, determination, and a passion for problem-solving.

The commitment to training stems from a deep-seated belief in the potential of those who will carry the torch forward. I want to be part of shaping a workforce that embraces challenges, understands the value of time and loyalty in problem-solving, and contributes to the continual evolution and success of the logistics field.

As the pages of this book turn and the narrative of my journey through the intricate world of logistics unfolds, I find myself at a juncture where a sabbatical beckons. The decision to take this pause, a deliberate hiatus from the fast-paced rhythm of the logistics landscape, is not an endpoint but rather a punctuation mark in the ongoing story.

The chapters so far have been a testament to the dynamic nature of the logistics profession—its challenges, triumphs, and the unwavering spirit required to navigate the complexities. The decision to embark on a sabbatical is not a retreat but a strategic pause, a moment to reflect, recharge, and recalibrate.

As I temporarily step away from the hustle and bustle, I anticipate that this intermission will not only provide the opportunity for personal growth and rejuvenation but will also serve as a vantage point from which to envision the next phase of the journey. The narrative of logistics is one that never truly concludes; rather, it evolves with each twist and turn.

The excitement to see where logistics will take me next remains unabated. This sabbatical is not an exit but a deliberate detour—a chance to explore new perspectives, gather fresh insights, and return with renewed vigour. The journey, after all, is an ever-unfolding story, and the upcoming chapters are pregnant with the possibilities that await on the other side of this intentional pause.

As I embark on this sabbatical, I carry with me the experiences, lessons, and resilience accumulated along the way. It is a moment of reflection, a deliberate pause, before the next chapter unfolds. The journey continues, and the anticipation for what lies ahead is laced with both curiosity and eagerness. Until the next page turns, I embrace the unknown with an open heart and a sense of gratitude for the chapters that have shaped this incredible logistics narrative.

www.ingramcontent.com/pod-product-compliance
Lightning Source LLC
LaVergne TN
LVHW091114150826
845673LV00002B/813

* 9 7 9 8 8 9 2 3 3 3 4 0 5 *